Yours Sincerely
C. Featherstone

Yours very truly.
Peter Featherstone.

REMINISCENCES OF A LONG LIFE.

BY

REV. PETER FEATHERSTONE,

Author of " Success and Joy of Life," etc.

LONDON :

CHARLES H. KELLY, 2, Castle Street, City Road.

Published for the Author—

BURSLEM :

JOSEPH DAWSON, Newcastle Street.

1905.

PREFACE.

Within the last twenty, or twenty-five years several persons have suggested to me, the propriety of putting on record some of the events which have occured during my long life.

Through my entire course I have had an instinctive shrinking from giving prominence to any personal matters : but as the *end approaches my heart is more drawn* towards any course which might magnify the grace of God, that has been so richly shewn in His marvellous loving kindness.

If anything is to be done in recording the Lord's goodness, it must be done without delay, having already passed my 84th birthday : or to speak more accurately, as recently taught by one of my children, my 85th birthday, as this may signify either the day, or the *anniversary* day on which one was born.

CONTENTS.

CHAPTER I.—CHILDHOOD.

THE earliest period of life I am able to recall, is when under five years old, I was sent off to the day school, a full mile each way. Along those rough and dirty lanes, my little feet had to toil day by day. At that school I remained for nine years. O how I wish the *excellency* of the training had borne some proportion to its *length*. But, Alas! Alas! whilst we were taught, parrot like, to repeat all the rules of Grammar, with great glibness and correctness, the Master never offered a word of instruction as to the relation of one part of speech to another, so as to relieve our puzzled minds for the time being, and to prepare us for future duties.

The School was in Fryup, 12 miles from Whitby, a beautiful dale, between Glaisdale and Danby. I do not know of one of my schoolfellows now living, one named Yeoman, followed the medical profession, became somewhat eminent; practised in Whitby, for many years with great acceptance, and there terminated his earthly career.

A very serious accident befel me, when about seven years of age; the end of a stick in the hand of a boy whilst

at play, caught the pupil of my left eye, and entirely destroy-
ed the sight.   The eye is very delicate, very precious,
invaluable, and much exposed to peril; hence, a wise and
gracious providence, has thrown over it, four tunicles or
coverings, so as to afford special protection.   Here at the
very opening of life, the sight of one eye was utterly lost,
but through this long roll of years, in dangers seen and
unseen, the one eye preserved has practically performed all
the duties of two, a special providence, under special conditions

> He, "Keeps with most distinguished care,
>   The man who on His love depends,
> Watches every numbered hair,
>   And all His steps attends."

Concerning God's ancient Israel, we are told that "He
instructed them, He kept them as the apple of His eye,"
(*Deut.* xxxii.-10).   For our strength and comfort, He assures
us, " He that toucheth you, toucheth the apple of His eye."
(*Zech.* ii.-8).

Through the above named accident at school, the Doctor
kept me in bed for a week, but all efforts to restore sight to
the injured eye were ineffectual.   From that time in the
year 1828 up to the spring of 1893, I never spent a day in
bed, either through sickness or indolence.   Since then, I
have had but two slight bronchial attacks, which kept me in
bed for a day or two on each occasion.   For temporal
mercies my heart is very full of gratitude to my Lord and
Saviour whom I love and serve, " He daily loadeth me with
benefits," (*Ps.* 68 19), to Him I say, " How do thy mercies
close me round."

I am very thankful to have very pleasant recollections of
my maternal Grandfather, Thomas Breckon, of Glaisdale,

where he spent a long life, finished his course with joy, and where his precious dust awaits the resurrection morn.

In connection with Methodist agency, the gospel was first preached in Glaisdale in the spring of 1784. While on an evangelistic tour, a messenger of the cross, reached this dale, and taking his stand in the open air, preached the gospel from these words, "Sow to yourselves in righteousness, reap in mercy," &c. (*Hosea* x.-12). Many flocked to hear, and the word was accompanied with power to the heart of Mr. Breckon, who was a man of thoughtful mien, prudent habits, and a yeoman of considerable influence in the place.

The heart of my Grandfather being in this way moved for the reception of Gospel truth, he was ready to open his door for the preaching of the word, but a very determined opposition was offered to these *strange proceedings* by my Grandmother. Having however won the favourable regard of the husband, these Methodist Evangelists quietly proceeded with their prayerful characteristic earnestness until at length the strong prejudices of Mrs. Breckon yielded to the force of truth.

After this they united with the Wesleyans, and their house became at once the hospitable home of all the preachers who visited the dale. The same generous entertainment, in the same dwelling, was, without interruption, continued by their only son, Thomas Breckon, Junr. He was converted to God in his youth, and through a long life, gave many practical evidences of his attachment to his Master's cause. Among the rest was that of presenting a large plot of ground adjoining the Wesleyan Chapel in Glaisdale, as a burial ground.

For a period of seventy-one years, he enjoyed all the advantages of Christian fellowship with the Wesleyan Community. In the early part of 1869, in the 90th year of his age, "He slept in death, to rest with God."

This hospitable dwelling and farm were owned for many years by the late Thomas Featherstone (my eldest brother) whose integrity and generosity were proverbial, and whose death at the age of 83 years, was as beautiful as his life had been. This same dwelling is now in the occupation of T. Featherstone Thompson, and has been known as an "open house" for more than 120 years. The present host and hostess have the greatest interest and pleasure in sustaining the record of rare hospitality in the roll of the generations past.

Now allow me to refer to an era in early life—the opening of my heart to receive the Saviour's love, in my thirteenth year. This took place in connection with a sermon preached by the Rev. Henry Richardson, January 19th, 1834, from the words "Choose you this day whom ye will serve" (*Josh.* xxiv.-15). Such had been the influences of the Spirit of God, and a Godly home, upon my tender heart, that I had been restrained from outward wrong, but my sense of sin arose from my want of love to Him who loved me, and gave Himself for me, and when the love of God was shed abroad in my heart by the direct witness of the Holy Ghost, which gave me a sense of acceptance with God, then my heart leaped within me for joy. As I walked home a full mile along the solitary lane on a January evening, "all nature" seemed to rejoice with my forgiven soul. I could then heartily sing,

> "To thee, Thou dying Lamb,
> I all things owe;
> All that I have and am,
> And all I know,
> All that I have is now no longer mine,
> And I am not mine own Lord, I am thine."

Everything connected with the dear old sanctuary in the dale, which witnessed my natural and spiritual birth are still very precious to me.

The most decided conversion, and in the earliest period of life that I have known, was a little girl, nine years of age. This was in connection with the last service I conducted before going to my first circuit. She was the child of devoted parents who had instructed her in the truth of Holy Scripture. She also took rapt delight in an illustrated copy of Bunyan's *Pilgrims' Progress*, so that her knowledge of God's method of receiving sinners was very distinct. On that memorable Sunday evening her sorrow was turned into joy, and her young heart "filled with the peace of God, which passeth all understanding." Through the roll of years she has adorned her profession of Christianity, shewing herself a "pattern of good works" in the varied relations of life. She is now the widowed mother of nine children; seven are married, one son and one daughter remain with her on the farm, at Wild Slack, Lealholm, trying to soften the sorrows of her widowhood.

Allow me here to say how firmly I believe in the conversion of children, and young people, and not in the notion of "growing up" into a new nature, and peace with God.

When the devout Jews in their captivity sat down by the rivers of Babylon, they wept when they remembered Zion. Although they were far away, their remembrance of the delightful services they had enjoyed in the old Sanctuary in Jerusalem, produced in them an undying attachment. For the expresssion of such joy, they employed the most ardent language. " If I forget thee O Jerusalem, let my right hand forget her cunning, let my tongue cleave to the roof of my mouth, if I remember thee not, if I prefer not Jerusalem above my chief joy (*Ps.* cxxxvii.-5, 6). Let me lose the power of speech, the most distinguished feature of my nature, if the prosperity of the cause of God is not at the top of my joy.

It was in the old Sanctuary where I found peace with God, that I first met in class, conducted by my own father, Mrs. Ingram, widow of the late Rev. Jabez Ingram, and their oldest daughter, "Sarson" (then "little Jennie") of literary fame, and who for many years employed her able pen to maintain righteousness and truth. These two still survive, the Mother "in age and feebleness extreme," the daughter in very feeble health,   It was here I attended the Sunday School; I still hold and greatly value a Bible, presented to me for substantially repeating the No. 2 Conference Catechism, which knowledge has served me well through life.

The congregations which assembled in that old Chapel in Fryup are as distinctly before my mind, as if of yesterday. I see in what was then known as the "singing pew," my venerable father; in the front of the gallery sat George Raw, distinguished by a large head of bushy jet black hair, father of the Rev. J. F. Raw, who has had a most honourable course as a

Wesleyan Minister, and greatly beloved in all his circuits. He retired from the Ministry five years ago, and has found a quiet retreat at Danby, in the house built and occupied by his highly esteemed parents. I also see very distinctly the familiar form of such men as Michael Thompson, John Dowson, John Chapman, Matthew Leng, Richard Burrows, and many others who were upright men, and valiant for the truth.

I cannot forget, and must not fail to mention the remarkable Lovefeasts which were held once a year, during the summer months, in the various dales of the Whitby Circuit These meetings commenced by a short service on the Sunday morning at 10 o'clock, the congregation was dismissed, but re-entered by the examination of the quarterly ticket. The Lovefeast was at once begun, and continued about five hours. I never found in these meetings any reluctance to speak, on the contrary two, three or four persons would rise at the same time to testify of the Lord's goodness to them. The meeting concluded, the friends were invited by farmers and others to a meal of marked hospitality combining dinner and tea. Then followed the evening service at 6 o'clock, when the Chapel was usually crowded. The Lord's people were full of faith, love and holy expectation, and it was generally a time when numbers made a surrender, and joined themselves in " Covenant to the Lord."

But you ask, what is the state of things now? Well, there has been a gradual toning down, and the old fashioned Methodist Lovefeast has lost much of its fervour. Lovefeasts are still held in the summer, commencing at 2 o'clock in the afternoon, when friends from great distances gather to enjoy the meeting.

The cultivation of family religion in the generations past, has had much to do with the maintenance of the Methodist form of Christianity in those dales which now to a large extent, constitute the Danby Circuit.

A cousin of the late Sir William Atherton, Solicitor General, after a few weeks spent in Glaisdale, gave to me the testimony that she had never seen primitive christianity so beautifully exemplified as in that dale.

When I think of the mercy, and distinguished loving kindness of God to me, in childhood, youth, and through lengthened life, I think I may say, the remembrance of such mercy has been in my mind and heart, *day by day* for a number of years past.   When I think of weaving the web of my early days, I am specially thankful for the influences of home in early life.   If the regularity and reverence with which the Bible was read, and family worship conducted are calculated rightly to impress children, then our first impressions were right impressions.   If the regularity with which we were taken twice on a Sunday, along those country lanes for divine worship form right habits and tastes, then ours was a favoured home.

The earliest recollections I have of my father, are, that he was cramped with rheumatism. from which he never found deliverance.   Although his affliction was so constant and painful, yet with his trap and pony, he went Sunday by Sunday, and frequently twice a day, to the house of God, because such worship was the delight of his soul.

I was one of nine children, all of whom from 12 to 14 years of age, heard and obeyed the Saviour's call to discipleship, and became members of the Methodist Church.

These have all entered the heavenly home, except one brother, the next younger than myself. He has been in Canada more than 50 years, and on February 1st, 1905, celebrated his "Golden Wedding." He has not been favoured with personal and family health in his home to the extent we have, but probably on that account he may receive a brighter crown, for "Whom the Lord loveth he chasteneth."

CHAPTER II.—Youth.

In my fifteenth year, my father bound me for 6½ years apprenticeship to Mr. John Anderson, of Whitby, the leading family Grocer in the town. Our hours of business for five days in the week were 13, from 7 in the morning till 8 in the evening; on Saturdays we had 15, closing at 10 o'clock. During 8 months in the year, the apprentices were not allowed to leave the premises, without consent from the Master. That restriction however was taken off from May to August inclusive.

The Master's arrangements during the eight months might be regarded by many to day, as a system of intolerable slavery. It was not however felt to be so by some of us, having free access to the best Library in the town, we found books which enabled us to cultivate a love of reading, this was fraught with many advantages.

The impatience under restraint and guidance, by many young people at the present day is not a hopeful sign. To spurn parental authority is the highway to ruin. These years of my apprenticeship were a sharp test of my early piety, but my feet were firmly on the rock of truth, and my whole being under the constant eye of the loving Father, in order that I might dwell with Him, constantly enjoying His friendship.

Now, that I was distant from home influence, from the immediate glance of a father's eye, and a mother's love, my father had spoken to a friend of the family, an old leader and local preacher, asking that he would kindly keep "his eye upon me." This he did for a number of years most faithfully. He induced me to attend cottage prayer meetings, read a portion of scripture, and give a few words of exhortation, then for a long time sought ineffectually to induce me to try to preach. At length I felt so ashamed of declining time after time, that I asked, when are you next appointed to Egton? He mentioned the day, I replied, well now, in order to convince you of what I am already thoroughly satisfied, I will meet you in that homely building, then you will know that I cannot preach. My loving and persistent friend had been morning and afternoon to two more distant appointments, and I walked 6 miles to meet him for this evening service. At the close as our faces were turned homeward, he said, "I hope you will not doubt any more now." Notwithstanding all my trepidation and confusion, I could not reply to his question in the same way I could honestly have done two hours before.

About 12 months after this, I preached my trial sermon from, "Who gave Himself for us," &c. (*Titus* ii.-14), in Wesley Chapel, Whitby, a Chapel opened by John Wesley himself. I was examined before the Local Preacher's Meeting, by the Rev. Joseph Raynar, and accepted as an accredited Local Preacher.

May I specially commend to young men, self knowledge self control, self mastery, I learnt in early life to clip the wings of expectation, and thereby prevented disappointment. During my apprenticeship I never asked my master for any favour which was not granted with cheerful promptitude. In the course of life's experience, I have now and then had a five or ten pound note put into my hand, which always evoked a feeling of special gratitude to God, such acts to me, indicated a feeling far more precious than gold.

When one of Dr. Dixon's colleagues was about to leave the Circuit, he was telling the Dr. how many acts of kindness he had received from various friends; the old Minister paused awhile, then in a gruff tone, said "it is all a shadow, after a pause he said, but the shadow of a glorious substance, and that "substance is in Heaven."

One of my greatest surprises, and highest joy was when my Master giving me my Indenture, put upon it a five pound note. But perhaps that surprise and joy were exceeded when I was the guest of a Deacon of a Congregation Church, during a Wesleyan Conference, just on leaving, as he opened the carriage door, and put into my hand a cheque for nineteen guineas. I went to his house a perfect stranger, but was in heart greatly knit to him during the short acquaintance because of the heart interest he manifested in the Master's work. All the good in our favoured land, is not by any means confined either to the Anglican, or the Wesleyan Church.

During these early years in Whitby my memory carries me back to 1839, the period when the Centenary of Wesleyan Methodism was celebrated through the connection. For this purpose in Whitby, the President of the Conference, the Rev. Thomas Jackson, preached from "Joseph is a fruitful bough, even a fruitful bough by a wall, whose branches run over the wall," (*Gen.* xlix.-22). He also addressed a public meeting in the evening. Another of the pulpit celebrities who visited us in these days was "Billy" Dawson as he was termed on the afternoon he preached in Wesley Chapel from the text " The elements shall melt with fervent heat" (2 Peter iii.-10), and in Brunswick in the evening, from " He brought me up, also out of an horrible pit," &c. (*Ps.* xl..2). The effect produced on his audience was very marked indeed. A friend of mine who heard him much oftener than myself, said he never heard a preacher grip a congregation like Dawson.

After spending six months happily with my old master as assistant, I took a situation at Heywood in Lancashire. This step was taken with the view of general improvement in business knowledge. The change of life was certainly very great, on the average I gave 16 hours a day to business, with just sufficient time from the counter to eat, but none to rest, In order to leave the shop by 12 o'clock on Saturday night we had to close the door ten minutes before twelve, and allow the customers on leaving to pass through the yard. To be in bed by one o'clock of course required dispatch in all matters. I was usually at the prayer meeting at 7 o'clock on Sunday morning, and then went forth to preach the word. Many of my appointments were 6 or 7 miles distant, as Heywood was then a part of the Rochdale Circuit Now facts of this kind, I would not mention, except in the hope that the reader may with myself, be stimulated to magnify the grace of God, and give him all the praise, for the way in which he has sustained my health, kept alive my soul, and given me great joy in proclaiming the glorious Gospel.

" Praise, O praise our God and King!
Hymns of adoration sing ;
For His mercies still endure
Ever faithful, ever sure."

During my business life in Heywood, I was associated
in the same establishment with Mr. Richard Bentinck, he
was a young man without school training, but of remarkable
resources, and by sobriety, integrity and activity, he has
made his mark in commercial life.   He retired from the
grocery business and took up the profession of auctioneer
and valuer.   He occupied rooms in Lord Street, Southport
from 1860 to 1895, and by his quick perception, ready wit,
and facile speech gained great influence in his calling,
whereby he secured considerable wealth.   A few years ago
he built and furnished for himself a charming residence at a
cost of several thousand pounds ; to-day, whilst I am writing
this line, he is celebrating his 85th birthday in Cavendish
House, Woodville, near Southport.

Having a short holiday in August, 1844, I went to visit
my dear father, and other relatives in the dales around, and
also to see a few old friends in Whitby.   Business matters
were freely and fully discussed, and the wish generally
expressed that I would settle in Whitby; several openings had
been previously named there, but my own mind seemed
always to find some objection.   From the very decisive way
in which I had refused to entertain the idea of the ministry,
no one mentioned it, except my father.   As we "bade adieu"
he simply said " Then you have not any thought that the
Ministry is your right place."   I replied, " Not at all, father "
The ministry was then quite foreign to my thoughts and plans.
Whilst in the train returning to my situation, the impression
came, directly from God, with a strength of conviction previously unknown to me.   *Whatever your love of business, and
your projected plans for the future, you will have to give them up
and go to preach the Gospel.*   For a week I treated that convic-

tion as a Christian person ought to treat a temptation from the Devil trying to occupy the mind with other things. The mind however, was so absorbed with the one thought, that I could find no rest by night or day, so I wrote to my old friend in Whitby, who had watched over me with so much fatherly care, and had so persistently induced me to preach, telling him of my journey in the train, and my restless experience through the week. He replied immediately saying " that during my visit he had never adverted to the subject of the ministry because of the decisive way in which I had years before refused to entertain the idea." He said moreover, "whatever course you may ultimately pursue, talk the matter over with the Superintendent Minister for your own peace of mind." From this course I shrank, but through the force of circumstances, was constrained to yield. Waiting for an opportunity when I could see the Superintendent alone, I had no sooner mentioned the subject than he said, " I was simply waiting for a chance to name the matter to you, several friends in Rochdale have recently said to me, they thought God intended you for the work of the Ministry; that is also my own view. Let me advise you not to reject, but cherish the thought, and leave yourself in the hand of God and of His Church."

Between this interview, and the District Synod in Oldham Street, Manchester, there were eight months. On account of the unfurnished state of my mind, and the length of business hours, I thought it very improbable that the Synod would recommend me, but for the sake of peace of mind, I resolved to act on the counsel of my friends. The day before I had to preach, and be examined, a most remarkable omission on the part of the Superintendent Minister came to the knowledge of the Synod, and they had seriously to consider whether or not they should receive the Candidate for examination. As it was not in any sense the Candidate's fault, they decided to let the matter proceed.

On the 18th of May, 1845, I preached in Oldham Street Chapel, at 6 o'clock in the morning. One of the three appointed to hear me, was the Rev. George Osborn, D.D. The Synod recommended me to the Conference, and the Conference sent me to the Didsbury branch of the Institution. I went the same day from behind the counter, to my study in the College, where I spent three eminently happy years, as helpful for the work before me, as they were happy in themselves. Now under these conditions, you can readily believe that whatever might have been my experience in the work as to comfort or discomfort, success or failure, I could never have doubted that God appointed me to the position.

How the conviction came in the train with such suddenness and strength remained for many years a profound mystery, at the time, I was not praying or even seriously thinking what course I should pursue. When in August, 1844, I was taking leave of my father, and he wished to know if my mind was at all drawn towards the work of the Ministry, and I answered so decidedly in the negative, I believe that he then had the impression that God intended his boy to leave business, and go to preach the Gospel, but he was always so afraid of any human element coming in between God and the soul of the preacher, that he would not do more than ask the question, "The secret of the Lord is with them that fear Him, and will show them His covenant."

My father saw that business arrangements were proceeding, and no ear was open to the work of the Ministry, his lips were closed to human ears, so he resolved to lay the whole case before the Lord in prayer. He asked if it is the Lord's will that *the business door might be blocked, and the door to preach the word might be opened.* In answer to such prayer the Spirit of truth, love and power, spoke to me with a voice which could not be mistaken. A week of perplexity and restlessness sends me to my old friend in Whitby, he counsels me to speak to the Superintendent Minister in Rochdale, this advice is reluctantly taken. As soon as the matter is named to him, he says that his own mind, and the minds of the leading friends in Rochdale are at one on this subject, and that for my own peace of mind, "I must not be disobedient to the voice from heaven."

Prayer is certainly among the reasons by which the great Father above is found marshalling events guiding his loving children with his eye, and by his own heavenly influences, *in a few days changing the whole current of life, which in its flow of sixty years has had peace, health and blessing most happily united.*

Will the reader pause for a moment and help me to magnify the Lord, and exalt His name together for His marvellous loving kindness?

CHAP. III.—DIDSBURY COLLEGE.

May I now ask the reader to go with me in thought to Didsbury, on Friday, September 11th, 1845. There I found the Rev. John Bowers, Governor of the Institution, Rev. John Hannah, D.D., Theological Tutor, and Rev. W. L. Thornton, M.A., Classical Tutor. The following year the staff was augmented by the appointment of Rev. Benjamin Hellier, Assistant Classical Tutor. Here were found 36 young men closely associated, consisting of 13 entering on their third year, 6 on their second year, with 17 fresh men; we were very similar in age, but differing widely in temperament and habit, with one common calling to guide and stimulate us. We had before us the most responsible and honourable vocation that can engage human thought and effort. The association was to myself both pleasant and profitable.

Soon after entering the College I formed an intimate and, undying friendship with John Payne James, from the Penzance Circuit, we were in heart closely knit together, like one soul in two bodies. It was a love that cannot die.

> " Friendship ! mysterious cement of the soul !
> Sweetener of life, and solder of society,
> I owe thee much ! "

That friendship gave a sweetness and success to our daily studies. The evening was usually spent in private by the students preparing for the classes of the following day. James and I always worked together. Tea over, without any loss of time, we went to one or other of our studies, turned the key, knelt down to ask God's blessing upon our Latin, Greek, Hebrew, or other subjects as the case might be.

It is said of Dr. Arnold, of Rugby fame, that he was once so troubled by the change he felt in coming from the death-bed of one of the boys, to the school work, that he resolved to make the latter more really a *Religious* work, and from that time he always offered prayer before the first lesson in the sixth form, over and above the general prayers read before the whole school. It was an attempt to make the common work sacred, by doing it in a religious spirit and to the glory of God. So our prayer, evening by evening, greatly assisted our daily work, and our spiritual life.

Frequently during our first year of residence, we had talked and prayed about the blessing, which came with "the full assurance of faith," the perfect love of God in the soul.

During one of our Quarterly fast days, when ordinary studies were suspended, a spirit of general expectation was awakened among the students, by quiet conversation together. On the "fast day" we assembled in groups of 8 or 10 in separate studies. The gracious Spirit divine came down with glorious power, and about half of the men were able to testify in the language of Charles Wesley.

> "'Tis done ! Thou dost this moment save,
>   With full salvation bless ;
> Redemption through Thy blood I have,
>   And spotless love and peace."

After this, the increase of enjoyment and power were very manifest, as our accounts were given on the Monday morning of the wonderful seasons of blessing on the previous day. Entire and abiding surrender to God, entire and firm trust in Christ, with the maintained victory over sin by the power of the Holy Ghost, were the true secret of a happy and successful life. What a preparation those Didsbury years were for a short career of less than four years in Circuit work, and what a preparation those Didsbury days, with their sanctified friendship were for my lengthened service, James could not have been more devoted to the Master's service, if he had known how soon the " happy toil" would terminate.

The Conference of 1848, appointed Mr. James to Hayle, in Cornwall. During his three years there, our correspondence was frequent, and to myself very stimulating and helpful. The Conference of 1851 was the time for our ordination to the full work of the Ministry. Mr. James met me in Whitby; thence we proceeded to Newcastle-on-Tyne, where the Conference was held. Our much beloved Theological Tutor, Dr. Hannah was President (the 2nd time) and John Farrar the Secretary. I had taken the, liberty of writing to the Minister responsible for " Homes " saying that Mr. James and I had been fast friends for years, and that if we could be accomodated under the same roof, the privilege would be highly esteemed. This request was kindly granted, and we found hospitable entertainment with the Chapel-keeper at Gateshead Fell. We walked day by day the 3 miles, slept in the same bed, and had a delightful opportunity of adding (what proved to be) the closing link to that golden chain of friendship which had been so much blessed of God. Conference over, the two young preachers parted, not to meet again on earth.

With our ordination vows fresh upon us, we resumed our happy toil. Mr. James was appointed to Cardiff, under the

Superintendency of the late Rev. William Appleby, which relationship had been happily sustained the three preceeding years. Here, as in his first circuit, he was "highly esteemed in love for his work's sake." Almost idolized by the people whose spiritual welfare he laboured so assiduously to promote.

He was naturally a man of sweet spirit; and when the grace of God wrought in him, and upon him, the result was a beautiful and spiritual manhood. After a few months' labour, about the end of March, the strain of work and a severe cold resulted in inflamation of the lungs. Rest and change were recommended, and for this purpose he went to Cornwall to visit his widowed mother and the young lady to whom he was engaged shortly to be married.

While in company with his former Classical Tutor, the Rev. W. L. Thornton, between Bristol and Hayle, he ruptured a blood vessel. At first it was thought that with great care he would rally, but rapid consumption of the lungs followed, and in a few weeks the hope of recovery had to be relinquished. But through extreme physical debility and blighted hopes, he was wonderfully sustained and greatly blessed.

The friends who saw him in his brief affliction, were, one and all, constrained to magnify the grace of God in him. Mr. Davies said to him, " Well Brother James, do you find Christ as precious as you expected ? " he promptly replied, " except in the depths of eternity." In possession of this peace —perfect peace, he continued to the end, about 7 o'clock in the evening of June 10th, 1852. he sang distinctly the hymn, commencing—

> "Jesus to Thee I now can fly,
>   On Whom my help is laid ;
> Oppressed by sin I lift my eye
>   And see the shadows fade." Hymn 393.

About two hours afterwards he entered the land of "Rest, eternal life." He was a beautiful singer, and was accustomed to act as our precentor in College. We think with grateful joyous hope of the prospect of meeting at the Saviour's feet. and of ascribing honour and praise, glory and power, to Him who hath "loved us, and washed us from our sins in His own blood." Looking at the last moments of such a victor, you ask,—

> " Is that a death-bed where the Christian lies ?
> Yes ; but not his,—'tis death itself that dies."

The late Rev. Wm. Appleby, his Superintendent for nearly four years, says of Mr. James, he was a perfect and upright man, "the most perfect man I ever met with." How blessed is the privelege of close fellowship with God ! When we are *in* Christ—partakers of His nature, sharers of His excellency ; then we can magnify the Lord together and exalt His glorious Name. When the believer is *one* with God *in* Christ, then whatever the Sovereign will of God appoints, he can perform ; whatever he is called to suffer, he can say, "Not my will, but Thine be done."

Here is a young man 30 years of age, in the 4th year of active ministerial service ; the immediate prospect of a happy marriage, his heart full of love to God, and with tenderest sympathy for all whom Christ died to save, delighting to preach a Gospel which tells of salvation from all sin, and for the whole race. In a few fleeting weeks his hopes are blighted, his purposes are broken off, and yet, blending with the darkest night, is the dawn of the brightest day, and he feels Christ as precious as he ever expected Him to be, "except in the depths of eternity."

My thoughts still linger within the Academic Grounds of Didsbury ; these reminiscences are sacred and very

precious to me.   One of these mementos is a " Ministerial
Album," which I very much prize, and contains an entry
from each Tutor resident in the College, in June, 1848.
The original composition and selections from choice
Authors are frequently expressive of leading features in the
character of the writer.   Out of the four Tutors and thirty
six Students, only four are now living.

The Rev. Samuel Lord, a gentle, faithful, loving soul,
who found a quiet resting place in California, twelve years
ago.

The Rev. John Reacher, though of short stature, is a
truly noble soul. Also the Rev. Benjamin Smith, who,
like myself, is a native of the Whitby Circuit. He is the
author of several works, such as " Vice-Royalty," " Sun
shine in the Kitchen," &c., &c.   These works, in connection with his faithful service as a Minister of
Christ,   have enabled him, through lengthened life, to
exert over many, a healthy and uplifting influence.   I have
had the pleasure of occasional correspondence with him ;
about twelve months ago, he told me he had been
preaching from the text, " I have rolled up like a
weaver my life," He will cut me off at the loom " (Is. 38, 12).
I have since, with great interest and profit, preached from
the same passage.   Mr. Smith was appointed for a second
term of service to Macclesfield, and was Chairman of the
District.   He has passed through very sore bereavement,
in the death of his dear wife and his two only daughters.
For service in the Church of God, they were a model
family.

As to the men of my own year, who entered the

College in 1845, for some years Henry Haigh, William
Hirst, and myself, were the only survivors, all Yorkshire
men.   On retirement, Mr. Haigh settled in Bath.   About
four years ago, he had a very serious accident, after which,
for 2½ years, he was unable to leave his room; I
frequently corresponded with him during this sad affliction;
his faithful daughter did all in her power to relieve the
burden which pressed heavily upon him.   He waited
patiently, but *longed* for release, which came in October,
1903.   Now the last link with Didsbury men, who entered
in 1845, has been broken, William Hirst, after a very
honourable and successful career, retired to Brixton Hill,
15 years ago, and in his 85th year, has just passed to
his eternal rest.

> " Life's work well done !
> Life's battle well won !
> Now comes rest."

Before leaving Didsbury, I may just say that one of the
rules, during my time of residence, was, that no Student
was at liberty to enter into a " matrimonial engagement."
That restriction I observed literally and honourably.   I was
much in the position of a " Candidate" under examination,
who claimed freedom, having simply made a " few silent
observations."   While in my teens, a young lady, who was
a very diligent collector for Foreign Missions, asked me to
become a subscriber, to this I assented, by and bye, the
impression took hold of my inmost nature, that if I should
ever be in a position to marry, I should seek the hand and
heart of this collector.   The thought simmered in the mind
for years, but was never allowed to boil over, or find any
kind of outward expression.   On leaving Whitby, I asked
the Collector if she would allow my name to remain in her

book, and I would remit quarterly, as I had previously paid. Out of this grew a little friendly correspondence, not exactly restricted to once a quarter,—this was continued during my residence at Didsbury. Here, I ought to say, the parents knew what the daughter did not know; and with parental thoughtfulness, they looked after my best interests. Liberated from the happy toil in Didsbury, where we were taught the lessons of industry and economy in full measure, I hastened to the familiar house in Bridge Street, Whitby, and there formally made and sealed the long anticipated engagement, which gave me great joy.

CHAPTER IV.—DENBY DALE, 1848-50.

After a very happy vacation, on the Friday before the last Sunday in August, 1848, I started for my first Circuit, Denby Dale (Huddersfield). What did I find there? Just the kind of sphere I should like if I were receiving my first appointment at the approaching conference. But how much better I should like to discharge all the duties of the office! I found there a small, but beautiful dale; near the top of which stood, on a slope, the Wesleyan Chapel.

"Beautiful for situation truly!"—In immediate connection with the Chapel was the Manse. The Minister in charge was Rev. James Bate, just entering on the 41st year of his ministry. He was a widower, a middle-aged working housekeeper, and I a lodger, constituted the varied Trio From the window of my study-cum-bed room I saw a field of beautiful golden grain bending to the breeze, and ready for the sickle.

We had then in the Circuit, 10 or 11 Chapels, with 5 or 6 preaching places or cottages. The return of membership in 1848 was 594; in 1904, 451. Possibly this difference may arise from the loss of those preaching places and cottage services near the Dale, they were to us a source of considerable strength, and great interest. Many of our members were hand-loom weavers, in their own dwellings. Nothing seemed to delight the people more than, at the close of the little service, for 6 or 8 of them to stay behind, detain the young preacher, and draw him out in conversation about Bible truth. and the state of the work of God in the Circuit. They were upright, stalwart, noble witnesses for the Truth, and taught me some useful lessons, as to how I might " roll up like a weaver my life." Instead of the plain Chapel. where the Sunday School was conducted, and the largest congregation for the day assembled in the afternoon, now I understand they have one of the most beautiful Chapels in the West Riding, and everything in keeping with it.

My Superintendent was a plain, sensible, quiet man, he would not disturb other people, if they would leave him alone, and he had very little confidence that people would receive good counsel from him, which they very much needed. One morning at the breakfast table he said, well brother Featherstone, Mr. Wesley speaks of the great advantage of a daily cross. I cannot speak from experience of the advantage of a *daily* cross, but I am sure when I go to . . . . I have a monthly cross. This was a home where he received hospitality once a month. The lady in question was a great helper in the cause of Methodism, very clever, very outspoken, and sometimes very sarcastic. She was strongly opposed to both tobacco and beer so much so, that she would not allow them in her house, not even to the Superintendent Minister. Persuading myself that I had some little influence with the good lady, on my next visit to the house, I said, now Mrs. . . . . you know my views and practice too, on tobacco and strong drink, and if it were the case of a young man who might be your guest, I should quite approve your restriction ; but in the case of a senior man, who is so temperate, that he never takes either through the day, is it not a pity to deprive him of one pipe and one glass of beer at the close of the day?   With characteristic sharpness, she turned upon me and said, " why do you preach to old sinners, why not let them alone, leave them undisturbed."   Hence I found she was not to be moved, either by argument or persuasion, and that I must leave the good lady and my super to themselves.

In this model Circuit, as I have said, for a young man commencing, we had sufficient preaching and walking exercise to keep both body and mind in good, healthy trim, In working the Circuit, the Ministers, in turn, left home once a month, on the Sunday morning, preaching thrice. and walking 6 or 7 miles, remaining out, and taking service each night, Monday, Tuesday, Wednesday, and Thursday, after which, we had to walk 4 miles home. On the alternate fortnight, we left home on Sunday morning, taking three services, remaining from home for Monday and Tuesday, then walking four miles, or staying for the night if the Minister preferred. This statement is not made at the risk of a failing memory, I have the Denby Dale Circuit Plan before me, from November, 1848 to April, 1849. At this time I had the honour of the acquaintance of Dr. Booth, of Penistone, he was a senior man, skilful in his profession, and watched over me with fatherly tenderness. If the good Doctor had, in these latter days, been on this side, "the Jordan," how glad he would be to know, and how delighted I should be to tell him, that through the years of my circuit labours, I had never omitted one appointment through want of health. I should tell him how on acting on such principles as he approved, and the divine blessing, the result which followed, viz: plain food ; water pure from the spring ; and no strong drink in any form ; good air to breathe, and plenty of steady work to perform, my health had been wonderfully sustained. Dr. Booth, himself, when about 70 years of age, had a seizure of paralysis, but was marvellously restored, and lived some ten years in fair health.

Possibly in the better life beyond, these things may form basis for review, and thanksgiving to God for His great loving kindness.

In connection with the congregation at Denby Dale, I distinctly remember twin brothers, Isaac and Jacob Child. These men were so much alike, that I could only distinguish one from the other when both were present. But while in person, they so closely resembled each other, in their manner of life, they greatly differed, Isaac had never the good fortune to find a wife, and Jacob brought his *third* bride to my first Sunday morning service in the Dale Chapel. She was a very intelligent, Christian woman, a thorough "Help-meet" to Jacob, and a blessing to his family, as well as to many others.

Isaac Marsden, a well-known Revivalist, his brother Joseph, and their sister, Mrs. J. Field, of Skelmanthorpe, were a family highly respected, and well known through the Circuit.

As I write, I have before me a reminder of Mr. Holmes, of Ingbirchworth, a mahogany writing desk, it is so constructed that it can be used either in a standing or sitting position. For it I paid the reasonable sum of twenty shillings, it seems as good now as on the day it was delivered to me, and may serve the same purpose for generations to come.

Were I to allow my pen to run on, I could "a tale unfold" about our faithful office-bearers, but I forbear with only the mention of one or two. Our Circuit Stewards, Aaron Peace and J. Wigglesworth, were faithful men, but in those days they had not much cash to place at our disposal, and occasionally gave us tickets to get cashed when we went to the villages.

Among the Local Preachers we had Richard Wood, Zaceheus Lawton, G. Gelder, S. Peace, E. Bottrill, not to mention other men, who studied their sermons, and preached "the Word" with great power. An incident which occured at our first May Synod may be worth recording. The Rev. F. A. West was Chairman, a shrewd, faithful, man. He thought my list of "books read" too short to be satisfactory. They questioned my Superintendent closely, as to the diligence of my habits. The fact was, I was very frequently at work for hours in the morning, when the other inmates were asleep. The same room for study and sleeping served me well in one respect, my fire was laid the night before, so that after striking a match, I soon had a nice fire.

The following year, when my list of books was read, the Chairman said, "that is a great improvement on the one a year ago, so much so, as to be remarkable." "Will you, I said, kindly allow a word of explanation?" "In my first year, I was acting on the counsel of the

Didsbury Tutors, who strongly advised us, when we left College, to keep up our classic reading, the judgment of this meeting a year ago, caused me somewhat to alter my course." To this, no reply was made.

CHAPTER V.—GRANTHAM, 1850.

By the Conference of 1850, I was appointed to Grantham, my Superintendent was the Rev. Jos. Floyd, with the Rev. W. K. Skidmore second Minister. Through the agitation, which was so general in the Connexion during the previous year, a large number of the members in Grantham formed an opposition cause, which was carried out with great determination and system. The position in which the Superintendent was placed, was most painful and perplexing. Mr. Skidmore was a Minister of considerable ability, and died soon after leaving the Circuit, while yet a young man.

For the working of the Circuit, which was wide, though the country very beautiful, a pony and trap was kept for the use of the Ministers. Instead of driving alone, to some of my appointments, I invited a bright-eyed boy just entering his teens, to join me. That boy is now "Chairman of the Macclesfield District." Chas. H. Floyd is well known in our Church as a good preacher, a wise administrator in circuit matters, and specially expert in all that pertains to the office of the "Chairman of a District." I have very pleasant reminiscence of such families as the Hornby's, the Dixon's, the Cox's, the Threadgold's, the Christan's the Newton's, &c. As this was the closing year of my "probation," my head and heart were pretty full, still I wanted to do something to put fresh heart and energy into the faithful ones, who remained with us.

For a whole month I took tea (not afternoon,) in 28 different houses. In connection with Grantham, I hold in my hand a long and the most interesting letter I ever received. The writer had seen, in the " Methodist Times," some mention of my name in Grantham, in 1850. Learning that I was still living, he resolved to write and let me know that at that time he was a farmer's boy, in the service of Mr. Bailey, of Eaton, and he was accustomed to go through the fields, and open the gates for the Ministers. On one occasion he rode with me to an adjoining village for afternoon service. The truth gradually laid hold upon him, until he received a clear sense of pardoning mercy.

A few years after this, he and his brother emigrated to N. Zealand, the new settlement of South Canterbury. Here they stood alone, exposed to much persecution, but still held fast to their principles of righteousness, and God has blessed them in a most wonderful manner. He says, " when we landed, we had not £10 between us, now we have property worth several thousand pounds." In the town of Waimate, where he resides, he was the first Mayor in 1877, has been thrice elected, and held the office at the time he was writing. He feels that in their behalf, the promise has been signally fulfilled. " Them that honour me, I will honour." In this town of 1400 inhabitants, the Methodist have a good brick Church, and their own Minister. The two brothers, of the name of Manchester, have held all the offices open to laymen. The oldest daughter of my *young* friend, at the little village of Eaton, was married by a son of W. Shepherd Allen, Esq., and I had the pleasure of meeting her at Woodhead Hall, Cheadle.

I have already alluded to the Conference held at New-castle on Tyne, in 1851. There I was received into full connexion, and by ordination set apart for the work of the Ministry. The purposes and pledges of that day are still fresh in my memory. Without loss of time, I made my way to Whitby, where I was married to Christiana, the eldest daughter of Mr. Horne, (founder of the Whitby Gazette,) in Brunswick Chapel, by Rev. Robt. Newton, D.D., on Friday, August 22nd, 1851. The Wedding Breakfast over, after reading and prayer, &c., the Dr. took stage coach to Scarborough, 21 miles, to fulfil his remain-ing engagements for the day.

Dr. Newton had just completed the 52nd year of his ministry, but still retained his erect form, his broad chest, and well proportioned frame throughout, and his clear voice of wonderful compass, placed him among the very first of natural orators, who have adorned the Wesleyan Pulpit.

Instead of yielding to the attraction of the first great Exhibition, in London, we took a quieter course. On the wedding day, I drove the bride 30 miles across the moors, in my father's trap, to Ormesby, in Cleveland. We went to the farm house of a double cousin, a brother of the late Rev. Thos. Featherstone, who was, for 20 years, Vicar of Tynemouth. We returned by the same route, the follow-ing Tuesday, and on Friday, August 29th, 1851, started for Belper, our new Circuit.

CHAPTER VI.—BELPER, 1851-54.

My Superintendent was the Rev. Thos. Shaw, a young man only seven years older in the ministry than myself. Here we found the sad effect of the agitation, known as the "Reform" Movement. Only four years before, the Belper Circuit was divided, Ripley becoming the head of the New Circuit. At the time of the division, there were about 1000 members in each. On our entering, we found about 360, and in Ripley, 220. In consequence of this state of things, the Conference directed that my labours should be divided between the two Circuits. On the Sunday, when I was due on the Ripley side, I preached three times, and walked twelve miles. But these days I enjoyed and took no harm.

In the beautiful village of Duffield, our people had built a new Chapel, but the agitators took possession of it, as there was considerable debt upon it, and the trust deed not having been executed, our people did not contest the point, but returned to the old Chapel, which they were using as a school. In the year 1877, I went to take part in celebrating the centenary of the old building. It was very unsuitable as a place for public worship, but they struggled on, until about a year ago, now they have built, I understand, a beautiful Church, on which, I trust, the divine blessing will rest for generations to come.

Although through the Circuit, the societies were
" minshed and brought low," those who remained were of
one heart and soul, they gave time, money, and enthusiastic
service without stint, and the Lord prospered the work of
our hands, so that by the end of the first year, the Ripley
Circuit was prepared to take a 2nd Minister. The Rev.
Thomas Timms was appointed ; amongst us at Didsbury,
he was a perfect picture of physical strength, and yet, by
an affliction of, at most, three days, his hopeful career was
suddenly terminated.

> " So blooms the human face divine,
>   When youth its pride of beauty shows ;
> Fairer than spring the colours shine,
>   And sweeter than the Virgin Rose."

The entire services of the 2nd Minister being now given
to Belper, the prospect of success was greatly increased,
and the year's experience furnished pleasing evidence that
God was with us.

The financial arrangements of Methodism at that time was,
to this effect, for newly married Ministers, in addition to the
stipend for a single man, he received for the 1st year, £24 ;
for the 2nd year, £35 ; for the 3rd year, £40.   Being responsible for his own house rent, rates and taxes ; the £100
a year, at the best reckoning, did not allow his money-chest to
overflow.   These were testing days for our Church, but as
a whole our people provide generously for the temporal
wants of their Ministers.   The Circuit Stewards, Messrs.
J. Longdon and A. Bell, were faithful men, and understood
the duties of their office.   Mr. J. C. Topham was a source
of great strength to us in this Circuit.   He was a fine
example of an upright, diligent, successful, christian

tradesman, and might well guide and stimulate those young men entering on life's business. He deliberately formed his plan, and drew out his own scale of systematic and proportionate giving. He commenced by putting aside one tenth of his profits, then steadily increased the proportion of giving, as his income increased, until, if it reached a certain amount, he would appropriate the whole of his income from business to benevolent and religious purposes. With God's blessing upon such a plan of working, he reached this, the highest point of his ambition. "There is that scattereth, and yet increaseth; there is that witholdeth more than is meet, but it tendeth to poverty."

Mr. Bailey, of Kilburn, was a rare example of a peaceful, healthful, and uplifting influence upon those who were both above and below him in the the social scale. As Manager of a large colliery, both proprietors and workers readily acknowledged his wonderful power for good. Many of the miners met in his large class, on one occasion whilst he was explaining, and enforcing upon his members, the duty and privilege enjoined in the text, "Then will I sprinkle clean water upon you, and ye shall be clean," &c., the Leader himself entered into the rest of "God's perfect love."

Let me further mention a *rare* example of large hearted liberality which was shown by John Holbrook, of Milford. John was a plain man, but very successful as a Class Leader and Local Preacher. On this Village Chapel there was a debt of from £200 to £250. The congregation worshipping there was poor. John promised to give £100, if, amongst them, they could raise the rest. This they were quite unable to do, therefore to accomplish the purpose on which the good man's heart was fixed, he gave a second £100, nearly all he had left. To justify this act, let me say that John was a bachelor, he did not live long after this was accomplished, but in the few years granted him, he worshipped with increased delight in the House of God which he so greatly loved.

A personal incident was so remarkable as perhaps to justify its being told. When John Rattenbury, in 1853, was in the height of his popularity, he came one week-day for the Anniversary Services of one of our village Chapels. His text on this occasion was, "The harvest truly is plenteous . . . that He will send forth labourers into His harvest." (Matt. 9-37, 39.) The Preacher so described the Heaven-sent, and the Heaven-endowed labourer, that I felt terribly impressed with my unfitness for the position. On the previous Sunday, at Belper, I had preached from "Awake, Awake, put on thy strength O Zion, put on thy beautiful garments O Jerusalem, the Holy City" (Is. 52, 1). I promised to give them a second discourse from the same text, the following Sunday. I was in the midst of my preparation for this, but after hearing Mr. Rattenbury's rousing sermon, I was, during the three days, quite unstrung. On the Sunday morning, I went to my service in that state of distraction, the *depressing* and *uplifting* influence seemed enough to rend the body asunder. Announcing the text, I adverted to the previous Lord's Day, and what I then promised.

I had no manuscript then, as now, it was quite out of my line. In my preparation I had four divisions, forgetting the first two, I stumbled on the 3rd. Having found my

way through that, and the 4th, I came to a stand! and asked
them to sing two verses. Just as the congregation resumed
their seats, "the Spirit who helpeth our infirmities" gave
me the first division of the sermon. I worked my way
through the early part of the discourse as best I could, and
concluded feeling compromised and ashamed. For the
next two days I kept as quiet as possible. On the Wednesday, I called upon one of our most intelligent Leaders,
and was scarcely seated when she said, "I have often been
much profited by your services, but I never heard you
preach as you did on Sunday morning." This was so
unexpected to me, that in my simplicity, I told her of my
fix during the service. She was of opinion that no member
of the congregation had any idea of my difficulty.

During the past year, we have been most appropriately
celebrating the centenary of the British and Foreign Bible
Society, but the grandest homage I have ever seen paid to
the "Word of God" was, when in Belper, 50 years before,
we celebrated the Jubilee of that noble society. It was
my great privelege to take part in a Public Meeting, held
in St. Peter's Church, and promoted chiefly by the Vicar,
the Rev. Robert Hey, who was a most Catholic spirited
man; and took the chair at one of our Annual Missionary
Meetings.

Such was the interest awakened, that at 4 o'clock in the
afternoon, all the s, millshops, and ware-houses were closed;
At 5 o'clock, in three different places, tea was provided and
served to 1,350 persons, in that small town of 10,000 inhabitants.

At 7 o'clock, the spacious Parish Church was crowded. The meeting was presided over by William Evans, Esq., M.P., and addressed by four Anglican Clergymen, all the Nonconformist Ministers of the town. Each speaker was limited to ten minutes for his address, the most breathless interest was maintained for three hours. These were not days of Ritualism and Semi-popery in the Established Church, influences so prevalent and injurious at the present time, leading away many from the 'simplicity of the truth. The Precious Word, " the Spirit's Sword," in opposition to all priestism, is the Book for all times and for all people. The conquests of the Word of God, when quiely read alone, have been glorious, and shall ultimately be universal.

> " We may be sleeping in the ground,
>   When it awakes the world in wonder ;
> But we have felt it gathering round,
>   And heard its voice of living thunder.
>   'Tis coming, yes it's coming."

CHAPTER VII.—HORNCASTLE, 1854-57.

The appointments made by the Conference of 1854 to Horncastle were, Wright Shovelton, Martin Jubb, and Peter Featherstone.

By *common consent*, never were three Ministers more suited to each other, or better fitted for the very peculiar work they had to accomplish. The dissatisfied ones in connection with the " Reform " Movement, had then for five years, occasionally attended class and public worship, but would not contribute anything, and by " stopping supplies," thought they would starve the Ministers into subjection.

Connexional Funds were languishing, and the Circuit debt amounted to £200. Mr. Shovelton had accepted an invitation to Horncastle, but the " first draft " of stations found him down for Bedford (John Farrar was President at that Birmingham Conference). He had a number of intimate friends in Bedford, and it was generally thought they must have Mr. Shovelton there. Messrs. M. Holdsworth and W. Green, Circuit Stewards ; G. Whitton, J. Rivett, G. Wright, and W. Sargent their valiant supporters, who knew well the situation, proceeded to Birmingham to storm the conference. Strong as was the influence in favour of Bedford, *by their six-fold cord of love, steeped in blood-earnestness, they fought like Spartons, and gained their point.*

Mr. Rivett is the only survivor of the brave six, and re-members very distinctly all the details connected with the crisis.   The preceeding nine years, Mr. Shovelton had spent at Oundle, Biggleswade, and Luton, all in the Bedford district, hence these Bedford worthies knew the type of men they were trying to wrench from poor Horn-castle.

I do not remember if Mr. Jubb was invited to Horn-castle, but I was not ; being engaged to St. Helen's, where a seven years man would have found a comfortable place, I was taken out, and a Minister, who had travelled fourteen years, slipped into my place.   Only in one other instance did I fail to obtain the Circuit to which I was engaged, hence my feeling is one of gratitude.   At Horn-castle, they provided me with a house, and a stipend of £70.   This they at once made £80, and the following year, £100.

After getting a fair start under these peculiar circum-stances, the first financial matter, to which attention was directed, was the debt of £200.   A Bazaar was arranged to be held, April 10th and 11th, 1855.   A large placard of four columns lies before me, the 131st item is " Two-hundred-and-a-half chip Kids."   At the bottom of the bill is the announcement for a sermon by Rev. W. M. Punshon, on the evening of the first day of sale.   He was then in Sheffield, and rose rapidly to great popularity, so that on this occasion he drew an immense crowd.   The Bazaar was closed during the time of service.

The result of this great effort was £444 4s. 4d.   The question was now asked, what shall we do with the surplus ? The noble-hearted men resolved that this should form a nucleus, out of which they would build two Ministers' houses, and the amount required was raised within a short time. Then Mr. Farr, of Minting, engaged to build a third house in Bardney, and simply desired interest for the money during his life time.

Mr. and Mrs. Holdsworth is remembered with great pleasure, they were at the head of a large household. In the business they had a number of young men, who were inmates of the house. In that company was the father of Dr. Henry Lunn. A little before my time, the Rev. Joseph Bush was an apprentice in that establishment, he, like many others, has done well. Mr. Holdsworth's house was on my way home, and I was always expected to call after the Sunday evening service and take supper, after which we had reading, singing, and prayer, thus a golden opportunity was afforded for getting the seeds of truth into youthful minds. In this home, we also met Master Edward, the eldest son of the late Rev. James Sugden. Grandma Holdsworth placed the little fellow (of five years, more or less,) on the table, and he repeated, with great distinctness and propriety, " The lives of great men all remind us," &c. From this home also sprang Mr. Thomas Holdsworth, for many years usefully connected with Cherry Street, Birmingham. Another pillar of strength in the Horncastle society was George Whitton, He was specially useful after he retired from business, and was a succsssful Leader of three large classes. At the quarterly visitation in those days, part of the Minister's duty was to call over the name of each member, and mark the quarterage.

There were several new members on trial. When I had read the other names I paused—the Leader said, " I think Mr. Featherstone, you have not finished the names," I replied, " yes, I have read all except those on trial," he said, " Is there any reason for not reading those ? Why should not contribution be a part of the trial as well as other things ?

We had also, another excellent man, William Sargent. whom I recall with pleasure. He also had retired from business, and spent a great amount of time in keeping the surroundings of the House of God orderly and beautiful. Time certainly not spent in vain. He also was a good Class Leader, and his members would sometimes give their Leader a little instruction. They told him, they very much wished he would conclude the meeting in an hour. Knowing the order in which they usually sat, and also something of their experience, for the following meeting he prepared a number of slips of paper, with a text of Scripture written, and as each member gave her experience, he put into her hand one of the slips, when the last had spoken, he took out his watch and said, " It is just nine." So in that quiet, and effective way he taught them that the fault did not rest *entirely* with the Leader.

One gentleman in this Circuit, Mr. Bratton, near Wragby, I love to remember for his rare courtesy. Whenever we took his Reports and received his subscriptions, he always thanked us, not formally, but most heartily for the trouble we had taken. If our friends who give their money to religious and benevolent institutions, would copy that example, it would harmonise more with fitness of thing, and make the duty of collecting a real joy. In another case, we had a Leader and Local Preacher, perhaps thirty six years of age, his home had become very solitary by the death of one parent after the other. I said to him, Mr. . . . don't you think it would be greatly to your advantage to get married? He said, yes I do, but I don't know where to find a wife. Well, there is Miss . . . of similar age, whom you have known all your life, what of her? Well, I never thought of her, I will consider. On my next visit to the village, six weeks after, the first startling intelligence I got was that he was engaged to Miss L. . . . It was not long before they were married, they were happier in married than single life, but unfortunately their union was not of long continuance.

I must not pass from this Circuit without the mention of a model Methodist family. Mr. Clarke's, of Wragby. It was a great event when Miss Louisa was to be married to the Rev. Aaron Edman, of Grateful Hill, Jamacia. The three Ministers and their wives, with a large number of friends went from Horncastle to be present. The family of the Clarkes were so knit together in love, that to lose Louisa from their circle was a terrible wrench. Every possible preparation was made for her outfit and future service, and the Divine blessing was constantly sought for the young Missionary and his highly prized wife. The accounts, which Mrs. Edman sent from Grateful Hill, respecting the naked, destitute children, greatly moved the hearts of her relatives and friends. One day, Mrs. Adams, of Torrington, and Mrs. F. . . . from Horncastle, met at Mrs. Clarkes, when the letters were being read; the question was asked, what can we do for the poor children? With characteristic promptitude and generosity, Mrs. Adams said, I will give a sovereign if Mrs. Featherstone and Miss Clarke will purchase material and make some garments for them. They applied to Mr. Rivett, of Horncastle, at once, who sold them a quantity of material on very generous terms, and with a little additional money they got enough to make 72 garments, that were speedily forwarded to Grateful Hill. Miss Clarke's Missionary zeal was well known. As to Mrs. Featherstone, she had, in her girlhood, a Missionary fire, which made her, in Whitby, an ardent and successful collector. When stationed in Derby, twenty five years ago, she assisted Mrs. Wiseman to form a Zenana Committee, and hold a meeting. That Society is still working. Even yet, in her eightieth year, the Missionary fire still burns, as she sits, hour after hour, at her table, contriving and stitching with unabated skill, and unwearied toil.

It has been my pleasure and honour to be associated with some able, and with many excellent men, in the work of the Ministry, but never did I stand by the side of one, whose example was so stimulating in all the duties of a Methodist Preacher, as that of Wright Shovelton. He showed far more heart in selling a poor man a shilling hymn book, than some half awake men do in preaching Justification by Faith. His heart was full of love, his eyes often full of tears and his countenance radiant with the joy of hope, as he told at the Preacher's Meeting how the alienated ones "got into liberty," when they gave their sixpence to the Worn Out Minister's Fund.

To induce the people, in a wide Circuit of 23 different places, to purchase and read Methodist literature, was an important part of our duty, and had much to do with maintaining the spiritual health and life of our people. Mr. Shovelton died in the height of his usefulness, when

only in the 30th year of his Ministry. Whilst Superintendent of the Lincoln Circuit, and Chairman of the District,
he went into one of the villages for a week-night service,
was seized with typhus fever so suddenly, that he could
not return home, and died within a day or two.

"Ceased at once to work and live."

Martin Jubb filled the niche of second Minister, and did
quite as well as either of his colleagues. He was a good
preacher, faithful Pastor, and served admirably the work of
the great Bazaar, being full of wit and humour. He continued in Circuit work for 49 years, retired in Belper, and
became totally blind. His fine flow of cheerfulness continued under this sore affliction. By a contrivance of his
own to steady his hand, he wrote letters to his friends, not
difficult to read. I had the privelege of receiving not a few
of these interesting letters, and found them much easier
to read, than some from correspondents with good sight.

The spiritual and financial prosperity of the Circuit
moved in beautiful harmony during the three years. Increase of members, 250. Increase in yearly and July
collection, £18 12s. 10d. At one of the Quarterly
Meetings, a Resolution was unanimously adopted to
raise 10 per cent for the Quarter Board. Nearly every
place in the Circuit raised the additional, and the full
amount was secured.

Amongst the Ministers there was not the slightest tinge
of envy or jealousy. We were one in mind, heart, and life,
and the same union of heart and purpose marked the
friends throughout the Circuit, we were glad in each other,
and specially thankful to God for the gift of the Holy
Ghost, whose presence ensured so much prosperity. As

the three Ministers had completed their three years' term, a " Valedictory Service " was arranged, tea at four o'clock, public meeting at six o'clock.   Friends came from nearly every part of the wide Circuit.   The amount raised was, I think, £50.   I will not attempt to describe the meeting, but simply say that in heart, we all sang,—

> " 'Tis Jesus, the First and the Last,
>   Whose Spirit shall guide us safe home,
> We'll praise Him for all that is past,
>   And trust Him for all that's to come."

CHAPTER VIII —BARTON-ON-HUMBER, 1857-60.

My Colleagues here were Robert Bond and Henry Kirkland, good " men, and true," but as diverse in physical form and mental temperament as you could have found in the Connexion. Here I found another agricultural sphere but the Wesleyan Farmers were rather more of the, Yeoman class. The Circuit extended about ten miles westward, and eleven to the east. All the Ministers resided in the town, and for the working of the Circuit, two horses and gigs were provided. The friends were very kind and hearty, and I have many pleasant remembrances of them, in which I must not indulge.

The Ministers appointed in my second year were John Philp and John Wood, (a) a younger man than myself. Henry J. Tomlinson, who has recently terminated a very honourable and lengthened life, was Secretary of our Wesleyan Day Schools, and greatly interested in the work of Education. He removed to Whitecross House, and almost immediately gave the Sewing Meeting ladies a tea. Not having had time to properly fit up the larger house, benches had to be used for the tea. I took the liberty of chaffing our Host, and asked if he called that a " House warming," &c. Why not have a proper " House warming," and give the proceeds to the present urgency of Fiji? He replied, " if you will get Mr. Tombleson to preside, I will." We shook hands across the table, the engagement was sealed. Mr. Tomlinson printed a letter of invitation, containing extracts about the urgency of help for the Mission work, and sent them to his friends. About forty accepted the invitation, Mr. Tombleson presided, the three Ministers, and of course our Host, gave addresses, the collection amounted to £70. The liberality on behalf of Foreign Missions, in my two Lincolnshire Circuits, has never been exceeded, if equalled, in any of my spheres of labour. In this Mr. Tombleson and his family nobly led the way. In addition to his annual subscription, he gave a special amount for Fiji, year by year. His influence was strongly felt in favour of practical and experimental Godliness. It was a rare occurence for him to be absent from the weekly prayer meeting.

The Missionary spirit still lives in the family. Dr. Bennett has recently sacrificed her life in the work, and Miss Tombleson, another Grand-daughter, is now working at Medak.

I record, with great gratitude to God, the way in which His Sovereign Grace was manifested in the patient suffering of the late Rev. John Nowell, retired Minister, in the closing years of his life. His whole frame was paralysed, yet still he showed much of the patience and gentleness of Him who was made " perfect through suffering." In reply to any enquiry, he would say, " Yes, believing on, hoping on, trembling on, rejoicing on." Blessed change when mortality was swallowed up of life, and death in victory.

John Philp, my Superintendent, was, as to moral qualities, a fine man, but his physical frame was far too feeble for the responsibility of a wide Lincolnshire Circuit. In the September of his second year, his health failed, and according to our Church order, I had to take the duties of his office. As this was only my ninth year of Circuit work, my youthful energies were taxed to the full, but to *help such* a brother, and to *serve such* a Circuit, was a work of love. We had also the additional and very valuable help of Mr. Wesley Brunyate as a Lay Agent. He was under twenty years of age, and recommended from this Circuit as a Candidate for the Ministry. He was distinguished for sobriety of mind, and gave promise of great mental strength. His soul was full of love to God and man. When the supply came for the afflicted Minister, we were indeed a youthful staff for a Circuit so extensive, but the Lord guided and strengthened us, and on the three years report, we had an increase of 138 members.

It was in 1858 that the disease known as diptheria first appeared in this country. In Barton it was very fatal, taking away all the children from some homes, in one house five died. From our home it took away our first-born, a bonny boy of six years.

CHAPTER IX.—South Shields, 1860-62.

Thomas Garbutt and I were the two Ministers appointed to South Shields. We were heartily received by the people, especially Mr. Garbutt, for having only left North Shields three years before, his reputation as an able preacher was well known. The two Ministers, for several years, had been united in close friendship, and the wives for the same time deeply attached to each other. The two families arrived on the last Thursday in August. Three weeks from that day, Mr Garbutt preached his last sermon. On the following day, he appeared to be suffering from a cold; on Saturday, much worse, and unable to preach on the Sunday. Monday was the Quarterly Meeting, and through the day my hands and head were so full of the business that I was unable to see him, and thinking he was only suffering from an ordinary cold, attended with fever. On visiting him early the next morning, he at once said, "My work is done," I replied, "you must not yield to an impression of that kind, the Lord has much work for you yet," "ah, no," he said, "I have felt through the night that the end is near; you will look after the mother and the children, and everything in the Circuit. Give my love to the people, tell them, the Gospel I have preached for twenty five years now sustains me." A Physician was sent for from Newcastle-on-Tyne, who consulted with the Medical Man in attendance, but before they could carry out what they decided upon, the spirit had fled. Towards that widow and her five fatherless children, in their sore affliction, we have exercised a brotherly and sisterly care. Her sad discipline of life only terminated a few years ago. How sweet is rest to such a pilgrim ! The very sudden removal of my beloved Superintendent filled our eyes with tears, and our hearts with poignant sorrow. We could only say in submission to the will of God, "I was dumb, I opened not my mouth, because thou didst it." When I think of the highly sensitive nature, the love of his heart, the tenderness of his home ties, and the suddeness of the Master's call, I magnify the grace of God, which enabled him calmly to give instruction, and to say, "it is all right." Inexperienced as I was, the whole care of the Circuit now rested upon me.

I had only one night in a fortnight free from engagements, and even that night rarely vacant. The chastened circumstances made all our hearts plastic. The people were kindly considerate, and most ready to co-operate in helping on the work.

It fell to my lot to nominate, in the March Quarterly Meeting, two young men as Candidates for the Ministry. One of them failed to pass the May Synod, the other, the Rev. James F. Pyle, has had an honourable course in the Ministry for forty four years, and has just now retired, residing in Portsmouth.

At Temple Town, we had a society, not wealthy, but one which gave their money and services very generously to sustain and extend the good work of God amongst them. On the eve of my leaving the Circuit, they arranged for a social gathering, viz : tea and public meeting, on which occasion a handsome present was made of a purse of gold. The very large number of subscribers, of small amounts was the most pleasing feature.

CHAPTER X.—NEWCASTLE-ON-TYNE, 1862-5.

The Ministers appointed to this Circuit were Edward Nye, John Roberts (a), Peter Featherstone, Henry W. Holland, and George Kennedy. The day after the Camborne Conference closed, twin children were borne to us. Even the short removal, at the proper time, was inconvenient, so that for a short period I did work in the two Circuits. After my first Sunday evening service in Brunswick Chapel, I walked home, eleven miles. This, in company with an old friend, was a pleasant walk. I did not wish to stay the night in Newcastle, and had never used the railway train on the Lord's Day. When I observe the inroads made, during the past forty years, upon our English Sunday, I am glad that I have, to the present, kept my own rule respecting Sunday trains, and now I think I shall be able to keep it to the end.

From the time of my entering the Ministry, I felt a special interest in two Connexional Funds, viz: the Theological Institution, and the Retired Ministers' and Widows' Fund; that interest led me to volunteer, to my Superintendent, to collect the subscriptions. Providence always, so far, favoured me, that I obtained a nice increase on the previous year. This was pleasing and encouraging to us both. But my greatest success was in Newcastle. When the late Mr. Bainbridge, a most generous man, able, and always willing to help, knew that I was going to collect, he said, " whatever increase you get, I will proportionately increase mine."

I only remember one application failing, that was in behalf of the Theological Institution. This call was upon one of our cultured friends, the very person I thought, who ought to favour this Institution. He hesitated, and I kept supply-ing additional reasons in favour, at length he said, " the fact is, I do not approve of these colleges—the men take the mould of their tutors, they lose their individuality and come out all alike." Yes Mr. . . . . . what a forcible illustration of your position you have in your own circuit to-day— Roberts, Featherstone and Holland. He blushed, but I did not get a subscription. I suppose if he had gone through the Connexion he would not have found three ministers more dissimilar.

> " Convince a man against his will,
> He's of the same opinion still."

I kept my Reports for many years, but cannot lay hands on them now, I think we got nearly double for this fund and for the Retired Ministers fund considerable more than double the previous year. Mr. Bainbridge paid his increased proportion with great pleasure. It was pleasing to find these fresh subscriptions kept up year after year. If the eye of any *young* minister should happen to read what I have written, on " *collecting* subscriptions " I trust he will consider and make trial of it. He will find great pleasure in the work.

Newcastle-on-Tyne supplies the finest illustration of the steady progress of Christianity under the Wesleyan form which I have known. Shortly after I left (forty years ago), the first division of the circuit took place. Now instead of one, there are five Circuits, instead of five ministers there are seventeen; and best of all instead of 1285 members, there are 4599. Let us rejoice and give thanks that the cause of truth and righteousness is prevailing, uplifting our fellow men, and bringing honour to the Saviour.

During the year 1863 we had in Newcastle some excellent services in celebrating the Jubilee of the Wesleyan Missionary Society. Our Deputation was the President of the Conference the Rev. George Osborne, D.D., the Rev. Morley Punshon, D.D., and Rev. Thomas Champness, who after seven years in West Africa came home in broken health, it was feared not likely to recover. He rose from his bed at noon, came down to the afternoon meeting for a *short* time, and spoke a *few* words. We thank God, that he recovered and that for forty-two years he has rendered such remarkable service to humanity and to Methodism. The services were of thrilling interest, and the sum raised in the circuit was £1756 5s. od.

The following incident may be given to illustrate the remarkable power of Dr. Osborn's memory. As we sat at the table of his Host I said, " may I ask Doctor, if you have any recollection of hearing my trial sermon in Oldham Street Chapel, Manchester, at 6 o'clock in the morning on May the 18th, 1845." He instantly said, " remember, yes ! I can give you the text from which you preached." " The Spirit itself beareth witness with our spirits, that we are the children of God." I replied, " well *I* remember both the occasion and the text, but that you should remember either, and especially the text is marvellous." We had not met during nearly the twenty years that had passed away.

In the following year 1864, my highly esteemed, and much beloved Classical Tutor was President of the Conference, the Rev. W. L. Thornton, M.A. In reply to a line of congratulation sent to him at Conference—he writes, at once in a note which shews his laconic style, and beautiful penmanship. "My dear Mr. Featherstone, many thanks for your congratulations, and more for your prayers. How greatly I need the latter." Observing the long established usage of the President, after his visit to Scotland, Mr. Thornton called at Newcastle to give us the advantage of his Sunday services. His Host and Hostess had invited for 6 o'clock dinner on the Saturday evening, some half dozen Anglican Clergymen, and several other friends to meet him. I knew Mr. Thornton was a model in conducting a conversation, but I never saw him to such advantage as that evening. It gave one pleasure and thankfuluess to have as our President, a minister who could shew such aptitude in a social gathering of that nature. He died during the year of his Presidency, I never saw him after that visit, but am looking with hopefulness to the meeting in "the House of many Mansions."

Some of my pastoral visits are very gratefully remembered, let me just name one. Annie B . . . . seventeen or eighteen years of age, perhaps the most sensitive, and reticent young person I have known—she could not speak to anyone, of her spiritual state, but was however greatly delighted when I read to her the Word of God, and prayed with her. As the disease advanced and her strength was diminishing, the solicitous mother said to a friend how greatly she should be relieved if Annie could give them assurance of her peace and safety. The friend replied " Annie is all right, and will very likely give you such assurance before she leaves you." And so she did—on Easter Sunday morning, she asked them to sing " Rock of Ages," when they had sung the first and second verses, they were unable to proceed, she said " sing it all, shout and sing " thus she sweetly " passed away " to her eternal rest in the triumph of faith.

I have felt it a privelege and honour to labour in all my Circuits, from first to last, but the noblest class of men as a whole, were in Newcastle. They were outspoken, but fair-minded, and of even balance---thoroughly loyal as Methodists, generous in their gifts, and ready for service, constantly " provoking one another to love and good works." I think with grateful joy of the noble army of those who " rest from their labours," but I must not commit myself to the mention of these names. Just as I write these lines, I am glad to see that Mr. T. H. Bainbridge was elected, yesterday, (July 24th,) a Representative to the Conference. He and the present Alderman, T. Richardson, were just commencing as Local Preachers. Mr. J. B. Bowes also rendered good service in the Psalmody as our Organist at Blenheim Street Chapel.

Sir W. H. Stephenson, J.P., D.L., I remember most distinctly, because he was my neighbour. The late Lady Stephenson we cannot forget ; neither her very excellent mother and sister, Mrs. and Miss Bond, who, for two years, were our invaluable, next-door neighbours, also the Misses Stephenson, who have, for some years, been exerting a most beneficial influence in religious and philanthropic enterprises. My friend in these early days, known as Mr.

Haswell Stephenson, was a young man of "Grit," "Go," and "Gumption." His powers developed, and matured rapidly, so much so, that whilst he was young, he was elected Mayor of Newcastle,—younger, I understand, than any other person elected to that office. That he was elected a 2nd, 3rd, and 4th time to the Mayoralty allows no room for anything to be said concerning his business abilities, or of the position he holds in the ancient City.

In my second and third year in this Circuit, the usual changes in our Church brought to us George Scott, D.D., and Samuel Wilkinson, both stalwart warriors in the cause. I also had the privelege of association with the Rev. J. P. Haswell, in his retired years.

That I should be invited to Brunswick, Newcastle, a few years after my "ordination" in that Chapel, I esteemed a great honour. My association with such Colleagues, and such Laymen, had a moulding and stimulating effect upon my future service. For this I heartily give praise to God.

CHAPTER XI.—KEIGHLEY, 1865-68.

While in this Circuit, our residence was in Haworth. The division of the Circuit did not take place till the year after we left. I had as Colleagues, Thomas Wood, John Brash, John Rhodes (B), and in my second year, Michael Johnson and Robert Davidson, M.A. Also glad to have the association of three " Retired " Ministers, Samuel Merril, Jonathen J. Bates, and Joseph Raynar ; especially the last named, having known him for many years. When I was in Whitby, he was Superintendent Minister, examined me, and heard my trial sermon as a Local Preacher. His daughter (Miss Raynar,) was a most excellent Christian lady ; our friendship with her extended over sixty years ; cultivated by correspondence, and not unfrequent visits. She possessed a well informed, and well instructed mind, and a heart full of love to the Master, whom she served so well. Whilst her health permitted, she was a diligent worker, meeting at one time three society classes, and for many years a most active member of the Dorcas Society. A very constant visitor of the sick, and the amount of relief she gave to the poor, none will ever know.

"Inasmuch as ye did it unto Me."

The Circuit Stewards at the time of our arrival were Messrs. J. Laycock and J. Redman, who gave us a very hearty welcome. The former had held office over a series of years, discharging its duties with great fidelity. In the course of the following year, I think, his long and useful life terminated, and he entered into "the joy of the Lord."

One of the important qualifications of a Methodist Preacher, is to be able to adapt himself to the various classes of society, with whom he has intercourse; to feel at home both in the cottage of the poor, and the drawing-room of the more favoured. To adapt himself to either village or city life. One of the sharpest tests in my own experience was, in leaving Newcastle, to fall in with the village life of Haworth. The people were thoroughly honest, but rigidly economical : keeping a keen eye on the chances of trade.

The morning after our arrival, I was walking down the steep street, which extends nearly through the village, a Butcher, standing at the door of his shop, called out, "Buy a good leg of mutton this morning." I thanked him for his courtesy and moved on. When I had been resident there about three weeks, one of our office-bearers meeting me in the street, modestly enquired, "How do you like us?" I replied, "I am surprised Mr.... that a man of your sagacity should have thought it needful to make such an inquiry, surely the way I have gone in and out amongst you for three weeks is a sufficient answer."—The good man seemed quite satisfied.

The Minister's house at that time was two minutes walk from the moor. To the whole family, the bracing air was refreshing, and invigorating ; in the first two months, September and October, the weather was delightfully fine. One of my pleasant moor walks was in company with the late Rev. S. Romilly Hall, a most faithful, and vigorous man. We were comparing notes as to our Circuit experiences.

He said, "When I first went to Southwark, London, the sights and sounds of sin were horrifying, and almost overwhelming; but familiarity with these surroundings took away the keeness of the feeling." We were quite agreed about the importance of guarding against allowing familiarity with the sights of sin, lessening our sense of the evil, or abating our efforts in trying to rescue the sufferers.

In Blenheim Street, Newcastle, I was President of one of our first Wesleyan Bands of Hope; but in Haworth, I found the Teachers in the Sunday School, indifferent, and some of them opposed to the formation of any such agency. I had to talk, reason, and persuade.—One of the senior teachers said, " I think I can keep myself from that evil." Yes! I said, Thomas, 1 think it *is* probable, with your serious mind and steady habits, you may never become a drunkard; but, what of the boys in the School as to the future? We knew that some of them came from the public house to school, on the Sunday afternoon. Before the end of my second year, we got a Band of Hope established, it rapidly strengthened. After I left, it became a flourishing institution, and I trust continues such, for the protection of our young people.

During my stay in Haworth, we had a series of remarkable revival services; they were continued for three months, without any outside help. Our Class Meetings were held every week, and as they were regularly met in private houses. one night in the week sufficed for these. Saturday night we kept for a Band Meeting, the other four nights for short addresses and prayer. We had many conversions of the bold, Bible type. One of the most notorious characters, was a man seventy years of age, a drunkard and a poacher, for the latter offence, he had been sent 19 times to Wakefield Gaol. When he first found his way to the services, he seemed in a dazed condition, and when he tried to go to the Communion Rail, he fell in the Aisle. But he got converted, and then shewed great aptitude and courage in exhorting his old companions to a better life. In our altered Church work, such a course of meetings would be very difficult to arrange, but the Spirit of God was present, to quicken and to save.

The late Sir Isaac Holden, M.P. rendered us excellent service as Circuit Steward. also in many other ways. In him we see how natural ingenuity and determined perseverence, with the Divine blessing, may raise a person from comparative poverty to great wealth. Mr. Holden took great interest in the training of our Theological Students, providing at his own cost, a course of Lectures on Elocution. To give completeness to his beautiful residence at Oakworth he spared no expense. His manner of living was plain and simple, and his walking exercises most regular and extensive. To get the resident minister by his side for a long country walk was a great delight to him. Towards the end of life his food consisted chiefly of fruits, taken with remarkable regularity, both as to time and quantity. He lived to the ripe age of ninety years, "He walked with God, and he was not, for God took him."

When I left the Keighley Circuit in 1868, there were 2,439 members. I look back with pleasure on the noble congregations in Temple Street Chapel, and especially the introduction of the new organ during my second year. What a change that made in our psalmody, and thereby the whole of the worship in the grand building. How few that were workers with us then now remain. My old friend, Mr. J. W. Laycock (then young) has done good service to Methodism. By his marked power, courage and impartiality he has by his pen, thrown light at critical periods of our connexional history. In other parts of the circuit we gratefully recall the Cloughs, the Smiths, and many others, but we must forebear.

CHAPTER XII.—LEICESTER, 1868-1871.

It is with peculiar pleasure and satisfaction, that I recall my entrance into the Leicester Circuit. We went on the Wednesday in the week of change, in order to be ready for the " Reception " Meeting on the following day. The late Rev. John Hartley was Superintendent Minister, and made the arrangements for the meeting, Mr. Hartley had given tea to all the office bearers in the afternoon, so as to afford an opportunity for hand shaking, and a few words of introduction to the new minister. This was followed by a public meeting, over which Mr. Hartley presided, and was nicely arranged throughout by addresses, with singing and prayer. Such a meeting greatly toned down the strange feeling on the first Sunday, from which some of us were wont to suffer.

Meeting the following morning with one of the office-bearers, a plain man, a Yorkshireman, I remarked how admirably the Superintendent had conducted the meeting last evening, " Yes he said, you will not find Mr. Hartley left-handed at anything." This good man who had carefully observed Mr. Hartley the two preceeding years, was strikingly correct in his homely simile. He was a model Superintendent, and an able minister of Christ. In giving his statement of work at the minister's weekly meeting, he would mention any special case of sickness he had met with. This had a wonderful effect upon his younger colleagues as to pastoral work, and in helping us to remember the sick. Physically our chief pastor was not strong, and his conscientiousness was seen by declining invitations for "social" evenings, in order that he might conserve his strength for "ministerial" duties.

It was the severence of many strong ties when Mr. Hartley left the circuit at the close of my first year. He had a quick eye, a sensitive temperament, a loving heart, hence the ties which united us were tenderly strong. As we parted on the railway platform he said, "You have been a great comfort to me." No words from human lips ever fell upon my ear which possessed the same amount of permanent, stimulating, strength as these. Because my beloved friend is now in the enjoyment of the "Higher Life," I may be forgiven quoting these words from his saintly lips.

In this life of change, God has placed one thing over against another. The gracious providence which removed the Rev. J. Hartley from Leicester brought to us the Rev. Edward Nye. I had joined him as his colleague a few years before in Newcastle-on-Tyne, and now he comes to join me in Leicester. To have him for a second time as Superintendent was very pleasant to me. He had a noble presence, good address, and was full of affection, always ready to accept help in his work, but very gracious in acknowledging the same. In the early part of his second year, he was seized with paralysis, affecting his limbs and speech whilst dressing in the morning. When I hastened to his room before eight o'clock, he began to describe the attack very calmly, and then with a touch of his natural humour he said, "You see even now I cannot speak properly. During nearly the whole of the Methodist year, he was laid aside. As the Conference was approaching, his medical man said he thought he might preach with safety, but not accept any Superintendency. A position at Barningham, near Barnard Castle was offered to him, where free from circuit care, he would have a quiet opportunity of preaching " the Word" to the same congregation. This position he accepted, and retained for seven years, and then peacefully finished his earthly course.

The President sent us as Mr. Nye's supply, a very excellent young man, the Rev. Henry J. Foster. His modest intelligence and devotion to the work before him, gave promise of what the future has brought, Most of his labour has been in City life, and in Bristol he spent nine years in succession.

When I left Leicester, in 1871, Humberstone Road had not been made a separate circuit, at that time there were 965 members, now there are 3,479. My old friend, the Rev. Joseph Posnett, was appointed to the Bishop Street Circuit, fourteen years ago. With the noble help of Revs. W. Bradfield, B.A., J. E. Rattenbury, and many other hearty workers, a glorious change has been effected, Mr. J. Coy and Mr. R. Mantle have each received from their Lord the welcome word "Well done." Also the devoted daughter of Mr. Coy who rendered such service in the Deaconess Training Institute. The work of the three was delightful, and their record is on high. I shall ever remember with devout gratitude to God, John Coy. Thirty seven years ago I made his acquaintance. In his earlier life he was connected in business with an unprincipled partner. Through this, the firm got into difficulties, and this distressed the soul of Mr. Coy very much.   As he was going along one of the public streets, this text was applied to him with peculiar suddeness and power, " If thou faint in the day of adversity, thy strength is small."   He stood still, and made a covenant with God, that if He would spare his life and health, he would pay every creditor what was due to him. He pointed out to me the very flag on which he stood when this covenant was made.   Like a man of mettle and perseverence, he went to work.   Before I knew him that matter was settled.   To the retail drapery wholesale business was added, and ultimately became a " limited liability " Co.   After all his generosity to religious and philanthrophic objects, he left £21,000 to be distributed. Surely we see the promise fulfilled, " Them that honour me, I will honour."

Mr. Joseph Roberts was a warm-hearted man, and very liberal supporter of Methodism.   His hospitality to the Ministers' was very marked.   It was a great disappointment to him if the minister after the Sunday evening service at Bishop Street, did not go to his house for supper.

Mr. Wm. Buckley was for many years a most faithful and acceptable Local Preacher and Class Leader.   On retiring from business, he resided in Syston, and there " sweetly slept in death to rest with God."

Mr. J. R. Rowe was another true servant of God, a diligent worker in connection with the Bishop Street Trust, he lived to advanced years, and then " fell on sleep."

CHAPTER XIII.—HUDDERSFIELD, (QUEEN STREET,) 1871-74.

This was one of the two Circuits to which I was appointed by the Conference, when engaged elsewhere. I did not take the place of a Minister engaged here, and therefore had a hearty welcome. The Revs. James Nance and Josiah Mee were my Colleagues. The former, a stalwart man, a good preacher, and a wise and firm administrator; he died in 1885, having had a sucesssful career. Josiah Mee was in his last year of probation, a brotherly young man, full of sympathy, thoroughly devoted to his work, and loved by the people. He found a suitable wife here, and afterward returned to claim her for himself. His Ministry is much of the type of the late Charles Garrett A sort of connecting link between him and Thomas Champness. He has laboured in several of our best Circuits. Twelve years in succession he remained in the Bolton District. Now in his present Circuit, Stratford, London, he is just entering on his *fourth* year. It is most gratifying to an old man, whose eye has been upon Mr. Mee through his entire course, to have seen him so cheerfully devoting all his powers to the uplifting of humanity, and the honour of the Master.

One of the families, which I remember in this Circuit with much pleasure, is Mr. Richard Haigh, of Kirkburton, his very excellent wife, and their numerous and intelligent family, Mr. H. was a man *sui generis*. He had striking peculiarities with manifold excellencies. In this quiet village he had a busy shop, embracing Chemist and Druggist, Grocery, &c. If he found a quiet hour in the afternoon, without many customers, one of his daughters would read to him while he was working away at his business. He had one of the choicest private Libraries that I have seen. The Ministers had frequently to walk home to Huddersfield, four or five miles, because the last train went too early for their convenience. Mr. Haigh was always ready to accompany us for the sake of the walk, and a talk about books recently read, and the current topics of the day; and then at my door, at half-past-ten o'clock, he would bid "Good night," and, with the cheerfulness of a lark, start on his journey home.

We had in our Queen Street congregation three spinster ladies, whom I must not fail to name,—Miss Sutcliffe, Miss E. Wood, and Miss Le-Resche. They occupied the same pew, and when able, were most regular in their attendance. The financial help they rendered was most generous, I should think quite equal to any three gentlemen in the congregation.

BRADFORD-SHIPLEY, 1874-77.

Up to this period of my Ministerial life, I had no difficulty in placing myself among "the young men," but when I got to Shipley, where I was the oldest of four, I felt very serious, and resolved, in the strength of grace, to do my very best in the responsible position. My Colleagues were Revs. Walter G. Hall, James Ritchie, and William Oldfield. The latter two already rest from their labours. The following year, Rev. Thomas Hind succeeded Mr. Oldfield. Three of us were new men, and they gave us a thoroughly good reception ; it was thorough, both in *kind and quantity.* We had to present ourselves in five different places, five weeks in succession, for Saturday afternoon tea and meeting. However, before the fifth meeting came, we felt we had had enough. It should be noted that this was some years before Windhill became a separate Circuit. I- looked upon the sphere as very compact, the most distant place not being more than three miles from my house.

Our Circuit Stewards were Messrs. John Denby and Edward Holden, men who served the cause of God faithfully and well. I have a very distinct remembrance of a visit to Mr. Denby's house, the day before he was to have a very dangerous operation, by Dr. Teale, of Leeds. We all knew that his life was in great peril, but he was so strengthened and comforted by God, that he met the trial calmly, went through it successfully, recovered wonderfully, and lived for a number of years in the enjoyment of much better health.

The Holdens were a great help to us. Good Mrs. Holden was a succourer of many in their distress, and full of " good works."

On entering upon my last year in Shipley, a circumstance occured, which shewed the thoughtful generosity of our people. The Superintendent of the Ilkley Circuit was called abroad for urgent Mission work. The President could not send as supply, a young man to such a Post.— Hence he wrote to the Chairman of the District, the Rev. John Hartley, asking if he could suggest anything to meet the difficulty. He thought, as we had four married

Ministers, we were fairly strong for our work. After he had talked with me, and our Quarterly Meeting was ust at hand, 1 asked him to come and state the case himself. He came and put it with inimitable skill, and then left the meeting.   With reluctance, but from a " sense of fairness," the meeting agreed to let the Rev. W. G. Hall go to take charge of Ilkley.   The President sent us as supply, the Rev. Samuel H. Hallam.   He preached well, visited with great diligence, and became very popular. A very significant indication of what his subsequent course has shown.

CHAPTER XIV.—Sheffield, Ebenezer, 1877-80.

Here I found a sphere of great activity and enjoyment, with an encouraging measure of spiritual and financial success. My Colleagues were the Revs. Jabez Marrat, Edward R. Edwards; the last named, at the end of the first year, was succeeded by the Rev. John Aldred. These were able and faithful men.

Our great financial work during the first year was to complete the Burngreave Road Chapel scheme. The cost of £13,000 far exceeded the amount at first calculated upon. In excavating for the foundation, the Contractor came upon a disused coal pit; this to him was such a serious business, that he could not proceed with the foundation except by measurement, and not according to the original agreement; this added a heavy amount to the outlay. Then the Trustees felt they could not reduce the cost of the building itself, and thereby spoil the Church, to be placed upon a prominent and beautiful site, such as they had secured.

Our Circuit Stewards were Messrs. John Dyson, J.P., and J. G. Shillito. They were men who understood well the relation between Ministers and their Circuit, and who faithfully discharged the same. Part of my correspondence with Mr. Dyson, before going to Sheffield had reference to certain alterations in the house, he said, " whatever alteration is needed for your comfort shall be done. Whatever interferes with your comfort will disturb our happiness as Circuit Stewards." That, I thought, is very nicely put, will it hold out? I am happy to say that through the three years it held out in detail, every word and deed.

John Dyson, as he was generally known, was an exceptionally noble man. He was a good and popular Local Preacher, knew his Bible thoroughly. To accomplish that, when in his youth, he went to work at six o'clock, he rose by four, to read and study the Bible, sipping his toast and water, prepared the night before, to keep him wakeful. He knew the polity of the Wesleyan Church far better than many of us Ministers. No Superintendent need fear about keeping on the right lines, if he had John Dyson in the Quarterly Meeting. He had a passion from his youth to understand Methodism in all its workings. As soon as ever he became a member of the Sheffield Carver Street Quarterly Meeting, (he told me himself) that he had walked the ten long miles from Thurgoland, and back home, without exchanging a word with any person, while attending the Meeting. His Magisterial qualifications on the Bench were proverbial, no specious putting of a false case could escape the detection of his keen eye.

Concerning the weighty scheme at Burngreave Road, some of our good men, of fearful heart, were ready to tremble, and others given to fault-finding did a little in that way. The Trustees however were whole-hearted men, " Men who had understanding of the times." They knew they had a difficult work, but they believed in their heart that it was a *good work*, which God would prosper. They kept enlarging their liberal subscriptions a second and a third time. We sought fresh subscriptions from likely and un-likely people and God wrought with us.

But as the time for opening the new Church approached, we were made to feel that our finances were not sufficiently matured. The Trustees assembled, kept looking at the matter from every possible aspect, until at a very late hour, (*I will not* say how late,) we very reluctantly passed a resolution to ask the ladies, by a Bazaar, to raise in our emergency £500. Good men love their wives, and some of these Trustees had so much kindly consideration for them, that they could not sleep soundly. One of them was sleepless, and he was astir early the next morning to say that he would give another £50 to avoid the Bazaar. Various other sums were promised, and it was decided the ladies should not be taxed with such an undertaking.

Our Trustees' Treasurer was William West Meggitt, who surpassed us all for cheerful activity and tact, promised one hundred additional guineas, from one hundred persons, not asking for more than one from each individual. By his suavity and gracefulness, he not only raised the sum promised, but secured £140 6s. 6d.

My recollections of the Dedicatory Services of the Burngreave Road Church are most distinct and refreshing. They extended from April 3rd to May 2nd, 1878. The first was conducted by Dr. W. Burt Pope, the last by Dr. W. M. Punshon; the first our greatest divine, the last our greatest orator. The younger man, the orator, died twenty four years ago, the older man lingered in "great feebleness" for many years, and his remarkable life only terminated two years ago. On the week day also, two celebrated Ministers from London favoured us with their help. Dr. Alex Raleigh (Congregationalist,) announcing as his first hymn, verse by verse with great effect, "Thou knowest Lord, the weariness and sorrow of the sad heart," &c. I am sorry this custom was ever discontinued amongst us. Dr. Donald Fraser (Presbyterian,) came directly from the Railway Station to the service; reaching the front of the Chapel, and putting his head out of the cab window, seeing the beautiful situation and the building, he exclaimed, "Well done the Methodists! This is not a Place of Worship in a back street! During the four Sundays in April, we had able Ministers of our own denomination, who rendered us good service. The collections amounted to £700.

The Trustees had already appointed a number of Sidesmen, who attended to the duties of their office with great diligence and tact, and thereby promoted the growth and stability of the congregation from the commencement. The Trustees honourably kept all the conditions of the Chapel Building Committee twelve months from the time of opening, also the return of £500 loan during the first ten years. Then five years ago, (although very few of the original Trustees were living,) these noble men resolved to enfranchise the land on which the building stands, and they have paid to the Duke of Norfolk £1,050. Having freed the building from debt, they could not rest unless they bought the land also, so that from that time it has been the Lord's freehold in the best and fullest sense of the term. It was a great honour and joy to me, that on the 22nd Anniversary, the Trustees invited me to take services on one of the Sabbaths, and thus to contribute a little to complete this noble work.

These original Trustees were men of true courage, who faced difficulties when they were very real, and on the darkest day they said to one another, " The God of Heaven, He will prosper us, therefore we His servants must proceed with His work." Four years ago, Burngreave Road was made the head of the Circuit ; Ebenezer having become a Mission Station.

At the close of our first year, the Circuit Stewards carried in the Quarterly Meeting unanimously, a resolution to increase the stipend of each Minister £20 per annum. We had in the Circuit a Supplementary Fund, to meet the expenses of keeping up the Ministers' houses, and other incidental expenses. When the Rev. J. Marrat and I left at the end of the three years, there was a balance of about £100 in this fund, and the same amount in the Circuit Fund. We however give the praise all to God. Those who had been doubtful and discouraged were now ready to sing :—

> " Away my needless fears,
>   And doubts no longer mine ;
> A ray of heavenly light appears,
>   A Messenger divine."

My remembrances in connection with the name of the late W. West Meggitt are the most precious and inspiring. He was strong in the " grace which is in Christ Jesus "—

which grace irradiated his countenance, imbued his spirit, sweetened his speech and moulded his whole life.   In him " the love of God was perfected " hence his love for the Word of God, the House of God, and the people of God, was full of inspiration to others.

Perhaps human eye never watched with more intense interest, or devoted zeal, the building of a House of God than West Meggitt watched the rising of Burngreave Road Chapel In its completion and dedication he had wrapt delight. The meekness and fortitude with which he bore his last, long and painful affliction, showed how close was his affinity to Christ.   The large company on the day of his funeral testified to the esteem and affection in which he was held—not only the members of his classes, his fellow worshippers, and fellow citizens—but even Ministers who had formerly laboured in the Circuit, shewed how in heart they were knit to their old friend, by travelling from St. Alban's, Birmingham, Beverley and many other places.   No less than eight took part in the service.

There were many other noble workers in the Lord's Vineyard whom I recall with great satisfaction and thankfulness and could easily enumerate, but I must forbear.

CHAPTER XV.—Derby, King Street, 1880-83.

In this old Methodist Circuit, I found a number of thoughtful, well informed, steady going people, who prided themselves in not yielding to excitement when the "New Preacher" arrived, notwithstanding they gave us a cordial reception, and were firm in their attachments. A little more kindly consideration one towards another, and a larger measure of enthusiasm in the Lord's work would have made the whole machinery work more smoothly and effectively.

My Colleagues were the Rev. J. W. Blackett, who preached good short sermons, and was succeeded by the Rev. W. Jeffries, who visited the people diligently.

Here I have not any successful Building Scheme to report, like Burngreave Road, Sheffield. I tried to reduce the debt on the old building at Ashbourne Road, but the friends did not touch it with generosity. My successor, the Rev. W. Ford, had the courage to try a new Chapel, and succeeded well ; that was doubtless the right course.

One of my most pleasant recollections while in this sphere of labour was the celebration of the Centenary of Wesleyan Methodism in the Derby Circuit. We were fortunate in securing the services of the Rev. G. Osborn, but when he arrived, he was extremely feeble. That night, and also the following morning, we could only hear him speak in a whisper. He was announced to preach in the Green Hill Chapel that morning, and was resolved to go and try. When he got into the work, he warmed up, and preached a most able and appropriate sermon from " Other men laboured, and ye are entered into their labours " (John IV, 39). The Dr. entered so fully into the Centenary celebration, that he expressed a wish to attend the Love-feast in the afternoon.

Towards the close of the meeting he rose and said, so many years ago, when I was twelve years of age, I attended my first Love-feast. Just as it was closing, I rose and said then as I say now, " My soul through my Redeemer's care " . . . . " shout His praise " (Hymn 528).

At the same Love-feast there was a fine old Class Leader, whom I had known thirty years before, and had come all the way from Belper to be present. The body of the Chapel was full, she rose in the midst of the assembly, and looking round with wrapt delight said, " Our Love-feasts have been going down of late, and I never expected to see such a sight as this." Then she gave us some sound Christian experience.

At the Public Meeting in the evening, the Venerable Dr. gave us a speech of more than a hour, elaborating the scripture argument of the duty and privelege of *Giving*. Thus ended a full and most interesting day, when the night before we feared our deputation would be obliged to stay in the house, if not in bed all day.

At Dale Abbey we had the smallest Chapel I have ever seen, and in it this amusing incident occurred.—We went to this small village occasionally on the Sunday afternoon, this visit of mine was about Christmastide, my text was "The Prince of Peace." Knowing that some of the people were *given* to sleeping, having announced my text, I said, now if the sermon is proportionately as short as the text, I trust none of you will feel any tendency to drowsiness I had not spoken two minutes when a worthy Leader called to a friend on the opposite side of the Chapel, "John, wake up Moses."

I have grateful and very pleasant recollections of the faithful services rendered by our Circuit Stewards, Messrs. Humphreys and Barlow, men who understood and discharged very steadily the duties of their office.

For all those who, twenty five years ago, were toilers with us in the Lord's Vineyard, who are still spared, we have a very pleasant remembrance, and for those who, through the death of Christ, have entered the Home above, we give thanks to God, and cherish their precious memory.

CHAPTER XVI.—ACCRINGTON, 1883-86.

In trying to summon any reminiscenses of this Circuit, my mind turns at once to the Circuit Stewards, Messrs. J. E. Lightfoot and William Smith (Spring Hill).

Mr. Lightfoot, in his eighty second year, was not only senior Circuit Steward, but the Mayor of the Borough. He had the honour of being the first Mayor, and was elected to that office several times afterwards. He was without exception the noblest senior Christian I ever knew. I think I am right in saying that Mr. Lightfoot was the first Mayor who held his annual Banquet without furnishing intoxicants on the occasion.

The Quarterly Meeting would not hear of Mr. Lightfoot giving up his Stewardship ; he would not consent to remain in office, unless Mr. Smith was his Colleague. This is sufficient testimony to Mr. Smith's efficiency in that office. He combined judgement and activity in high measure, and succeeded Mr. Lightfoot in the office of Mayor. The meekness and humility of the senior Steward was quite proverbial. I believe he was really puzzled to understand how a person with so little to commend him should have so many honours thrust upon him.

Being engaged to this Circuit, I was anticipating with much pleasure, the association of the Rev. Joshua Priestley, who was residing there as a Retired Minister, but his useful, uplifting life terminated rather suddenly a few months before I arrived. He was a Minister greatly beloved, and an author of several excellent books. His work on Mental and Moral Excellence, which I read in my early days, is among the most instructive and stimulating books I have known.

My Colleagues in the first year were Thomas Hackett and Samuel Fogg, after these, Charles A. Collingwood and J. Wesley Genge,—all good men and true.

Mr. Hackett was a very good preacher but his health was feeble, and he was accustomed to depreciate himself very unwisely. I reminded him that the trend of human nature was in that direction, and others would do quite enough of it. He had real worth, and must not undervalue himself so much.

My recollections of Alderman W. H. Rawson, the present Mayor of Accrington, are cheering and refreshing. While I was in the Circuit, I had ample opportunity of observing his manner of life, and have no doubt the counsel and example of his late Uncle, Alderman William Smith, contributed largely to the formation of his character. As a young man he was sober-minded, attentive to the duties of home, diligent in business, in all things, and at all times, a thoroughly upright Christian man. If his voice is heard in the Synod, or the Conference, there is always the right ring in his utterance. He would never follow impulse, and disregard sound principle. You may trust him that he will " Never go to law, for the wagging of a straw."

I am very pleased to remember that one of our young Local Preachers, some twenty one years ago, gave up his daily calling, addressed himself to study, and by undaunted

courage and unflagging energy, proceeded step by step
until he passed the final examination for the Medical profession, and is now Doctor Nuttall, practising in his
native town.   He is also a member of the Town
Council.

It is moreover a great pleasure to sometimes trace my oft'
repeated steps to Quarry Hill, and think of Mrs. Bunting,
a Model Mother to her fatherless children, as well as a
Model Christian Worker, and though I have rarely, if ever
seen them since I left the Circuit, still it is a real joy
to note, from time to time, " the good hand of God
upon them."

CHAPTER XVII.—TUNSTALL, 1886-89.

On entering this Circuit, we were very kindly received by the Circuit Stewards, Messrs. T. Clare and T. Burgess. These were two excellent men, who did their very best during the three years to sustain and extend the work of God. In entering this sphere of labour, we had not all the strangeness of feeling usual on going to a "New Circuit." Six months before we came, our son had introduced our long name by commencing business in the Market Square. This had very much to do with fixing my appointment.

About a fortnight before our arrival in Tunstall, a dark commercial cloud arose, which very much affected the whole Circuit. The Collieries and Forges of Messrs. Robert Heath & Sons were entirely closed at Kidsgrove, and a very large number of men, totally left without employment, moved away from the neighbourhood in order to obtain work. My Colleagues were Revs. C. S. Reader and Walter Lang. To help to meet the emergency the three Ministers gave quarterly subscriptions, and a large number of friends in the Circuit did the same This unfortunate state of things disturbed the financial working of the Circuit for years.

In reviewing, I might look upon this as the most laborious Circuit I have had, but I was happy in the toil. As I walked along the dark, dirty lanes with lamp

in hand, I would not have exchanged my position for
that of the Archbishop of either York or Canterbury.
The Chapels as a whole are good, and attendance at the
week-night services used to be very encouraging.

That which seriously disturbs the enjoyment of both
Ministers and Members is a lack of loyalty to the
Church, with which they have chosen to identfy themselves. Such loyalty should be found among Christians of
all denominations, common prudence implies that our
decided preference shall go for those with whom we are
identified.

I have a very pleasant remembrance of some who are
still active in the Master's cause ; but of a larger number
who have passed to the " Higher Life," such as the two
Stewards I have named, men with whom I felt in all con-
sultations and action, they had a heart interest in the
spiritual welfare of the Circuit. Also their associate and
my old friend, Mr. John Moulds.—As a Class Leader he
was instructive and faithful, as a Preacher of the Word, he
was full of enthusiasm and power.

The " Martinmas Tea Meeting " I recall with gratitude
because of the help it afforded, both to Local interests
and to the great Missionary enterprise. By the way, what
a contrast there is between the amount raised twenty to
thirty years ago, and the present, for the Foreign Field.
On taking up the report for 1878, I find the amount for
Kidsgrove is £30.—The last Report is £8 19s. 3d. The
former was the time when the Rev. J. F. Raw resided there,
and which a few still remember with most devout gratitude
to God. Now to think that we have had a Wesleyan

Minister resident there during these twenty seven years fills the mind with lowly shame and piercing sorrow. We have need with one heart and voice to pray, "Help, Lord, for the godly man ceaseth, and the righteous fail from among the children of men."

If the Minister had been taken away from Kidsgrove as some advocated years ago, then this result, by common consent, would be attributed to his absence. It would be a great joy of heart to me if this old Circuit of mine should put on the "strength of unity, and the beauty of holiness," then the right arm of the Lord would become "glorious in power."

CHAPTER XVIII.—LONGTON, 1889.

The Circuit Stewards, Messrs. R. H. Plant and J. Griffiths, gave me one of the heartiest welcomes I ever received. The very generous, not to say lavish expenditure in the house to promote our comfort, seemed to say in act, what a former Circuit did in word and deed. "Whatever prevents your comfort would prevent our happiness as Circuit Stewards."

Between Longton, Stoke, and Fenton, there were elements of discord which had been simmering for a number of years. I tried to melt them in the caldron of love, but I fear I did not succeed to any great extent.

We had in connection with the Minister's Society Class a number of elect ladies, who were a great help and power with us in financial matters. Mr. William Machin's Class for young men was the best I have met with in the whole course of my Ministerial life. In enthusiastic and steady work in the Master's Vineyard, he has few equals, and perhaps no superior. The Circuit Stewards have both passed "to the rest above," and many others, such as Mrs. Richard Hulse, Mr. Proctor, Mr. and Mrs. Edwards, of Stoke, whom I very gratefully remember.

CHAPTER XIX.—BURSLEM.—RETIRED LIFE, 1890.

If, when I came to Burslem fifteen years ago, I could have thought it probable I should have enjoyed the uniform health, so graciously granted, I should scarcely have taken the responsibility of asking the Conference to allow me to retire. Although I had been forty-three years in the Ministry, I had been so thoroughly happy amid the activities and toils of Ministerial life, that I calculated on less enjoyment. But in the freedom from Circuit administration, diminished financial resources did not awaken any concern.

On our entrance here, Ministers and people seemed as, with one consent in word and deed, resolved to make us feel that we had only come to a new Circuit. In quitting the " Chief Pastor's " position I had no aching of heart. That which I had enjoyed, and still longed for was to " preach the Word," and visit those who were physically and spiritually sick. For this work I found ample opportunity. Seven Sabbaths in the Quarter were appropriated to the Burslem Circuit and the principal Chapels in the Hanley and New-castle Circuits were opened to me, two sabbaths to the former and three to the latter. The remaining Sabbath was given to an old Circuit, or a Sister Church. On consulting my memoranda at the end of three years, I found I had preached twice every Lord's Day without a solitary exception. I do not say that I never went from home for a holiday, but on my holidays I preached. Now so far from working towards that result, I was somewhat surprised to ascertain the fact.

For several years after coming here, I took about two week-night services, with the frequent quarterly meeting of the Classes. For such opportunities of service, for bodily strength, and for a heart to enjoy it, I do this day thank my God. To Him I would give *all the praise.* I recall with great satisfaction, my visits every third Wednesday to Smalthorne. My custom was to go for tea to the house of my old friends, Mr. and Mrs. Kirkland, where I always found a hearty welcome. Between tea and service hour, I visited the people. and obtained a good knowledge, both of the society and congregation. Within four or five years of my first acquaintance with Mr. Kirkland, he was suddenly seized with affliction and passed away. He was an excellent Christian man, whose friendship I valued. Whatever he did, either in connection with business or the Church of God, "he did it with all his heart, and prospered."

A short time ago, I met in Hanley for the first time, a young Doctor who had heard about my years and manner of life. He said—" Now Mr. F., I should think through life you have been very particular, and lived by rule !" I replied not perhaps in the way you imagine Doctor. I have taken in moderate quantity plain food, as it has been set before me, water as beverage, not strong drink in any form, no tobacco or cigars. I had forty-three years in the full work of the ministry. during the first six years of "retired life" I did much the same amount of work. At the present time 1 preach once or twice most Sundays, so that plenty of work and little recreation with God's blessing account for my present enjoyment of life.

I recall with great pleasure the improvement at Stanfield. Our old friend Mr. Wilson, by consistent devotion kept together the class and little congregation in the modest upper room in Stanfield Road.

When the gift of land on which to build a new chapel had been made by the late Mr. Tellright, the foundation stones laid, and the Building opened and dedicated to the worship of God, the heart of Mr. Wilson "rejoiced with exceeding great joy." The warm-hearted and efficient services rendered both at the "Stone laying" and "The opening" by the late Rev. W. Wilson (Figi) of Macclesfield, were highly valued.

My recollection of change made at Norton-le-moor I name with great pleasure. Their former Chapel and School accomodation was most inadequate and incovenient, but now they have secured a handsome Village Chapel, kept in good order. By systematic, persevering and liberal efforts, they are reducing the heavy debt with which they have had to contend. Religious education and the saving purposes of Christianity are steadily advancing, so as to encourage faithful workers.

On an occasional visit to Sandy Lane, it is very pleasant to find a model place of worship, steady effort on the part of a few, and the Blessing of God, may they have the joy of seeing the Spiritual Church prosperous !

My "Class roll" in Burslem, consisting largely of senior people, has entirely changed. I find such names as Joseph Edge (the former leader) Thomas Blackshaw and John Longson. It was always a pleasure to have intercourse with such matured believers. Joseph Edge not only raised a high standard for other people, but also took the model for himself. Some of his workpeople very gratefully remembered for many years the pithy sentences he would use for their guidance in life. He was courteous, upright, and pitiful, having a heart to feel another's sorrow, as well as his own. I think about a year before his happy life closed, he had a paralytic seizure, which it was feared would prove fatal. A day or two after, I called to enquire after him, and was taken to his room, I said, well Mr. Edge, do you at this crisis find Christ real and precious? With his usual cheerful promptitude he said, "O yes! Jesus Christ, the same yesterday, to-day, and for ever." About a year after this, he died in great peace.

On that "Class roll" I have also the name of James Dean, with whom and his family I made a very pleasant acquaintance while living in Tunstall. for many years he was connected with our cause in Burslem, holding various offices, especially that of Chapel Steward. He removed to Stone—there I occasionally visited him, but when through family connections he removed to Lincolnshire, I had not the pleasure of meeting with him, and there a few years ago, he peacefully finished his course.

Another name, Mr. Arthur Dean, was well known in connection with the Wesleyan Chapel here, by the length of time he presided so efficiently, at the organ. His last affliction was long and painful; I occasionally visited him, and had the melancholy satisfaction of performing the last sacred rite of burial.

Mr. Blackshaw, and Mr. Longson both had considerable suffering in the eventide of life but they enjoyed communion with God, and fellowship with his servants. They both delighted to talk about the former Ministers, and the old Chapel in past days. Resting upon the great Atoning Sacrafice, they passed away.

Soon after we came to reside in Burslem in 1890, the Rev. C. H. Kelly now President of the Wesleyan Conference was visiting us, he said " whatever has led you to settle in this smokey place?" I answered, we have a son, our only son, spared to us, living in Tunstall. O, he said, "that accounts for it all." It is quite true that sensible parents live very much in their children, and will not *choose* to live far from them.

Having a fair amount of health and activity, I was able to render a little service to neighbouring circuits. To Hanley, Tunstall and Newcastle, I have been able to walk three or four miles on the Sabbath morning without adding to the fatigue of the day. Newcastle and Burslem have now obtained each an additional Minister so they require less help. The buoyancy and vigor of youth are as a matter of course preferred in the pulpit, to the sobriety of years.

For the late Mr. James Malkin, and his family I have a most profound respect. William Boulton, true as steel, and good as gold, such men as these and Spencer Lawton, one can only recall with devout gratitude to God. Their power for good in the work of the Church and in the Borough will never be known. "These all died in the faith."

With great interest I recall the name of John Holdcroft who died nearly seven years ago in his 89th year, and was at that time the oldest member of our Society. He loved the house of God and was very regular in his attendance. I have frequently talked with him about his early days in the Burslem Sunday School. He was the only person I have known who remembered the disturbance which arose, about teaching writing, on the Sunday, and other matters. His life was one of consistency and much activity almost to the end, and terminated in great peace.

The name of John S. Gardiner recalls a man of remarkable fervour, and devotion to the cause of God in the various offices which he held. So the name of John Oliver brings before us, a man of quiet habit, but who was a staunch supporter of the cause of God to the last.

Mature life ought to be something different to its opening, and old age to be brighter and better than the meridian, as it brings us nearer to Christ, and prepares us for " the better life." As our eyes close on " the dear ones " on earth, they shall open to behold " the King in His Beauty."

The changes which have taken place in our Wesleyan Polity since I entered Didsbury sixty years ago have been many and great—most of which I have heartily approved. Those who oppose changes in general are sure to be left behind, to their unhappy reflections. Wesley himself was not opposed to improvement of any kind. When some of his people objected to his changing one thing for another " he told them he was willing every day to be wiser than the last, and to change all arrangements that could be made for the better."

Jabez Bunting and James H. Rigg have both been able advocates for liberal changes in our polity " for the better.'

These recollections hastily sketched, and expressed in familiar style, I cannot expect to meet with approval from some into whose hands the booklet may fall. But whatever may be the manner of its reception, I shall not regret what I have done, because my desire was to bring honour to Him who through life has "loaded me with His benefits." My sense of humiliation is deep, because I have not reciprocated *such* mercies, in a much more adequate way.

Having learnt to trust with simplicity and confidence the "Father in Heaven" I find the lessons of cheerfulness and thankfulness flow. If glory, honour, immortality and eternal life are to crown such a life of mercies, it will simply be "heaven the reward for heaven enjoyed below."

I sometimes try to picture what the land of "Beulah" will be to the Methodist Minister, when he enters the "House of many Mansions." To revive, perpetuate and perfect the friendships formed between his faithful colleagues and the band of beloved fellow-workers gathered from twelve to fifteen circuits.

"The Lord reigneth let the earth rejoice, let the multitude of isles be glad thereof." "While I live will I praise the Lord ; I will sing praises unto my God while I have any being."

SOUTHWOOD BROTHERS,
118 HIGH STREET CREDITON

www.ingramcontent.com/pod-product-compliance
Lightning Source LLC
LaVergne TN
LVHW061219060426
835508LV00014B/1362